MANAGING TO READ

A WHOLE-SCHOOL APPROACH TO READING

£10-95p

Wendy Bloom

Tony Martin

Mick Waters

MARY GLASGOW PUBLICATIONS

Published by Mary Glasgow Publications Limited,
Avenue House, 131-133 Holland Park Avenue,
London W11 4UT

©Mary Glasgow Publications Ltd 1988

Typeset in Palatino and Optima by
Mathematical Composition Setters Ltd, Salisbury, Wilts
Printed in Great Britain by Hollen Street Press, Slough, Berks.

ISBN 1 85234 201 3 (school edition)
ISBN 1 85234 217 X (trade edition)

British Library Cataloguing in Publication Data

Bloom, Wendy
  Managing to read : a whole-school approach
  to reading.
  1. Great Britain. Primary schools. Students.
  Reading skills. Development. Teaching
  I. Title II. Martin, Tony, 1945–
  III. Waters, Mick
  372.4′1′0941

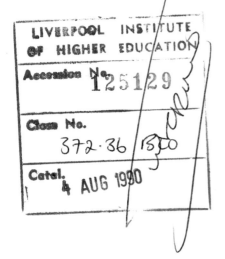

Contents

Acknowledgements

We would like to thank Carol Green for letting us use some of her material; the teachers and children who responded to our questionnaires; the heads, teachers, advisers, parents and children who answered our questions and shared and discussed their concerns with us; Betty Morgan and her class at Cranford Infants School for permission to include their *Nottiberky* story; and *The Guardian* for permission to reproduce their advertisement.

We would also like to thank Nancy Martin for the illustrations.

Introduction

This book is concerned with children learning to read. It is also concerned with schools and the ways they can best help to develop children as readers. Many books have been written about the teaching of reading, each with a different slant on this complex and often controversial area. The reading process has been analysed in great detail; the nature of written language has been expertly described. Much advice has been offered to teachers about what they ought to be doing in their classrooms. Today, perhaps more than ever before, arguments rage about approaches to reading with young children. Looking at the books and articles currently available, however, we believe that one of the most important aspects of the reading scene has been badly neglected: the process of actually developing reading in a school.

So many positive initiatives have floundered because the actual day-to-day managing of the reading curriculum has not been given proper consideration. If development is to be initiated and maintained, the issues which need to be addressed are as important as the approach to reading itself. Indeed they are crucial to the development of any curriculum area in a school. In the world outside the school gate, these same issues affect the day-to-day running of industry, offices and factory floors everywhere.

The aim of our book, then, is twofold. First, we want to share with you our own ideas and those of other teachers, parents and children with regard to reading. We hope you will use these to reflect upon your own practice. Secondly, we consider management issues of crucial importance to developing reading in your own school. The book therefore has been designed to be used by groups of teachers, either from the same or different schools. We believe it is by

1

discussion with each other that the best way forward lies. However, the book can also be used by individuals.

When we run workshops on in-service courses, the first activity we set up is for teachers to consider the qualities they feel they are trying to develop in the children they teach. These are not qualities tied to reading or whatever other area we are considering, but general, personal qualities. The question we ask is, "By the time children leave primary school, what sort of qualities do you hope to have developed in them?"

Every time we ask teachers this, the same qualities appear. The lists read something like this: happiness, independence, confidence, self-reliance, imagination, respect, ability to get on with others, ability to make decisions. Perhaps you could spend a couple of minutes deciding if these qualities correspond with your own ideas, and if you can think of any others.

We don't discuss the lists at the end of the activity, but put them away to be referred to later. If the focus of the course is reading, we now ask for a list of 'reading qualities' which children should take to the secondary school. Again, the same lists appear at meeting after meeting: love of books, enjoyment of reading, being able to read for different purposes, being able to read for information, critical awareness, sensitivity, ability to use the library, ability to choose books for different reasons.

These lists always elicit a general nodding of heads and murmurings of agreement. Clearly, then, they reveal what teachers are aiming at in their teaching. At the end of a day spent considering how best to help children learn to read, the lists are re-examined. We make two points about them. First, they serve to remind us that we are teaching children rather than the subject of reading. The ways we provide for children to develop their reading will affect the way they grow up, the sorts of people they will be. Secondly, development of the personal qualities which make up the first list depends upon the strategies we employ in our classrooms with regard to reading and other areas of learning. If we want children who are confident and self-reliant, what sort of classroom will best facilitate this?

Taking the second list, if we want children to learn to love reading and books, what should we be doing with them in our schools? We hope that this book will encourage you to reflect upon the way you approach reading. As teachers, we need constantly to bear in mind the two lists of qualities above. They should form the backcloth to your discussions about how you would hope to influence reading development in your own school.

Organisation In order to facilitate the use of this book by groups of teachers, we have included what we call TIME OUT at different points in and between chapters. Each TIME OUT provides an opportunity either for discussion about an aspect of reading or for a look at present provision or practice in school and classroom. In sports, the TIME OUT gives the team a chance to stop the game and consider future strategies, and we believe teachers need to stop the 'game', take a breather from the frenetic world of teaching and consider what they are doing. We have suggested the length for each TIME OUT, shown in the stopwatch that accompanies them.

No school exists in a vacuum, and so to begin with in chapter one, we draw attention to the issues which currently dominate the reading scene and to some of the pressures which affect teachers and the ways they work. Chapters two to seven consider a different aspect of reading and its management in schools. We examine reading through the eyes of the adults involved — teachers and parents — in chapter two, and then move on to look at the process from the children's point of view in chapter three. Chapters four and five concentrate on issues which affect development. In chapter six, we present practical ideas for what we believe to be a sound way to approach reading with children, and in chapter seven we explore what we mean by progress as a child learns to read.

Chapter 1

SETTING THE SCENE
Have you read any good books lately?

We are surrounded with print in our environment. We are members of a highly literate society. We need to be able to read all kinds of different material in different ways for different purposes.

We want to read novels, poems, plays, magazines, journals, newspapers, comics. Being literate is everyone's entitlement. This means both being able to read everything we want to read, and also enjoying the reading. Who is seen to carry the main responsibility for our level of literacy? Teachers!

Teachers in primary schools are well aware of this awesome task. Children are also aware of the vital importance of reading. Ask four- or five-year-olds what they hope to learn at school and the answer almost inevitably is "to learn to read". So with the vision of 'lifelong readers' on the one hand, and eager learners on the other hand, what happens in between? Teachers in classrooms up and down the country do their best to help children learn.

There is argument and disagreement about the best way to set children on the path to literacy. Different approaches are being followed, now usually based on new theories of language development. There are many new reading schemes and programmes being advertised. Parents are being invited to play an important role in how their children learn reading and writing. There are hundreds of new books, new writers, new illustrators.

All this goes on in education, but schools are not cut off from the rest of society. Education and literacy are often in the limelight. Messages and pressures come from many directions to influence or disturb teachers to a greater or lesser degree.

As teachers, you need time to look at things squarely, so you are not rushed into making changes nor into defending your position. Try to take some time out from the pressures and the 'busyness' of your day-to-day life with a class of children.

In this chapter we'll look first at some of the issues that are currently forming the national debate on literacy. Then we'll look at some of the factors that might be influencing you in your school. The current debate is like the scenery in a play: it forms the context in which the players operate. Usually it is mere background, but sometimes it assumes direct importance. Always in the foreground are the pressures that are part of teachers' everyday lives. They are always there, like wet playtimes. These pressures can work in two ways:

spurring on or inhibiting, encouraging growth and development or inducing resistance.

Change and development isn't easy. It's not likely to be successful if undertaken hastily. Schools are not islands, much less the teachers within them. There is a wider world that we need to become aware of and respond to in some way. Some debates about literacy are transitory, other debates recur.

This chapter will try to set the scene for the rest of the book. Before you can think about how or what you want to develop or change, you need to take stock of what is going on around you. This chapter aims to assist you to do just that, helping you towards awareness of current issues, debate and pressures from outside and from within your school. You need to take stock, too, of your own particular situation if you want to develop or change the approach to reading in your classroom or in your school.

Take a deep breath. Sit back and consider.

THE EDUCATION REFORM ACT

The part of this education act that has aroused most controversy is the proposal for National Attainment Testing for children at 7, 11 and 16. The three areas of the curriculum in which children will be assessed are the areas that will form the main part of the core curriculum in primary schools: language, maths and science.

The nature of the assessment will take some time to refine, so complex is the problem of formulating a realistic and worthwhile set of tests.

NATIONAL ENQUIRIES AND REPORTS IN LANGUAGE

see ref. 1 The Bullock Committee was the last group to look at language teaching in schools. *A language for life*, published in 1975, was the result. Many of its observations and recommendations were thoughtful and far-seeing, but it sometimes seems as if little has come of them.

see ref. 2 In the discussion paper 'English from 5 to 16', published in 1984, the proposed objectives for children at 7, 11 and 16 evoked many critical responses. There was much disquiet

7

but the principle has been carried forward into the Education Reform Bill.

The Kingman Committee was set up in 1986 by the Department of Education and Science (DES) to examine and give recommendations for the teaching of English in our schools. It was set the task of deciding how, how much and when children should be taught *about* language.

Teachers might find themselves in a conflict between their own understandings and experiences and the prescriptive directives and recommendations from the DES — not an easy situation to resolve.

DEBATE ON ILLITERACY

A report publicised in the national press stated that one in 10 adults sampled in 1983 admitted to having difficulty with reading or writing, many more with writing than with reading. Because the demands of our literate society are very high, people can be disadvantaged in their personal and public life by a low level of literacy.

We cannot seem to achieve universal literacy, even given that children are obliged to attend school for 11 years. This is a matter of great concern to primary teachers especially. How should such a worrying figure affect desire to change? How might current moves in reading affect long-term prospects?

'Falling standards' have long been a part of the national debate on education. Newspaper reports back at the turn of the century commented on a lowering of standards in literacy within schools and within society at large.

DEBATE ON THE ROLE OF PARENTS

The Education (No.2) Act 1986 brought much more influence to parents over their children's education. Parental choice of school has been given a much higher priority. Parents as the majority group of governors have increasing authority over the curriculum and the running of schools. Parents generally can call schools and teachers to account. The Education Reform Act 1988 allows a majority of parents voting to take the school out of the jurisdiction of the local authority. This is power in its strongest sense.

8

GRANT RELATED IN-SERVICE TRAINING (GRIST)

GRIST is a new way of funding and developing in-service provision for teachers, taking account of national and local priorities. Although the picture varies between Local Education Authorities (LEAs), the general outcome is that schools have more choice and more control over meeting their local needs. For the first time, every teacher will experience some regular in-service work.

DEBATE ON READING SCHEMES VERSUS REAL BOOKS

'Reading schemes versus real books' is a shorthand way of expressing the current debate on different views of the reading process and different approaches to reading. Theories of language development and of social and cognitive development underly the choice of texts and the choice of approach. There is a good deal of discussion about such questions as: What is a reading scheme? What makes a book a real book? What is the difference? Does the difference matter?

You may wonder what all the fuss is about. To you the argument may seem esoteric rather than real and important. After all, don't most children learn to read one way or the other?

Nevertheless, most teachers are aware of the current debate even if they are not already responding or wondering what they should do or think. This book will attempt to explain the argument fully in order to help you decide the best way for you and for the children you teach.

These, then, are some of the points and arguments being raised and discussed nationally, and providing a backdrop to the main action that takes place in schools and classrooms. These pressures exhibit themselves in different schools in different ways, and can make teachers feel that they are merely responding to demands or suggestions without the opportunity to think things out for themselves.

In primary schools with a 'broad and balanced' curriculum, teachers have to be knowledgeable and up-to-date in many different areas. Even for the most energetic and concerned, it is difficult to keep up. It is even more difficult to find quiet time for reflection and discussion and to bring everyone together over children's reading.

PRESSURE POINTS

Parents We often hear teachers say about parents:

We'd like to move away from reading schemes but our parents wouldn't like it. They are used to the structure of graded reading materials. They've got older children who learned through reading schemes. They'd think we were being too trendy.

Some teachers feel unsure about how they could explain to parents why they want to develop a different approach to reading, and to take them along with the idea. This is a real worry; but when schools make positive moves to explain to parents and involve them in the reading, they usually find a ready response.

Advisers Advisers are frequently heard saying:

How is your language policy developing? Do you think it would be a good idea to send someone on this course? Have you managed to appraise your reading material for racism and sexism?

Advisers' and teachers' priorities do not always coincide. Usually schools welcome the interest and help of advisers, but it can be quite difficult for teachers to admit to not having sufficient knowledge or expertise. This is especially true as advisers are more and more becoming inspectors.

Colleagues Other teachers in the school express opinions like:

...I've read this fantastic book/been on this really good course/seen this amazing school. I've got all my class doing it!
...I've been doing things this way for years now and I don't see any reason for change.
...We've read Frank Smith at college/been told that you can't teach children to learn to read. Why do we/Do you still use reading schemes here?

Although most teachers in primary schools have the responsibility for a class of children, they work with a team of teachers within the school community. Each one affects the other. Over-enthusiasm on the part of one colleague can seem charming and naive at the same time, but not always welcome. Proposals for a new approach can seem daunting and make us feel threatened that we may not be able to measure up. We may be established in more traditional ways that seem to have worked, and it appears unnecessary to take on what looks like just another idealistic venture.

Publishers We are bombarded with publishers' blurbs such as:

...a new reading programme which uses real stories and whole language to help children to read.

...a resource which helps you to plan for your pupils' reading development realistically, comprehensively and effectively.

Representatives of publishers will come to school staffrooms during the lunch break, or to local teachers' centres. Glossy catalogues advertise bargain all-in packages which look much cheaper than buying individual titles. Publishers of reading schemes are responding to recent thinking and emphasise their holistic view of language in offering an all-embracing language programme which takes care of children's reading, writing, talking and listening. Materials are based on a 'story approach'.

Parents have been targeted, too, with learn-at-home books. There has been an epidemic of these books in bookshops, supermarkets and newsagents. Some of the publications are lively and interesting, others seem to be little more than the drills-and-skills approach that we have moved away from in schools. Publishers are in the business of selling books and it follows that they will try to meet — or sometimes create — a trend.

We have tried in this chapter to give you a brief glimpse of the material debate that will always go on about literacy and how it is best achieved with children in schools. We have also looked briefly at pressures that are closer to home.

We have suggested in the TIME OUT activities that follow this chapter things to talk about to help you clarify your thoughts and become aware of the pressures and influences on you and your school.

11

OLD NEW DEMANDS

Think back over your career as a teacher. Try to identify a specific change that has occurred within your practice in the area of early reading. Note it down.

Can you remember exactly what it was that made you make this adjustment in the way you worked? There may be several answers; it may be a combination of factors.

Chat with colleagues and see whether the reasons that you have all made changes fall into any particular pattern. Were changes made because of head teacher pressure; research findings; trends; LEA decisions; resources; government acts; personal beliefs; working style? Try to remember whether you made the decision to alter your practice or whether you felt pressured into it.

Within the scope of chapter one, this TIME OUT is meant to encourage you to reflect upon the pressures that have influenced your career to date, and to put current debates about reading into some sort of perspective. As chapter one illustrates, teachers can find themselves in the middle of several interlocking debates, and it is important that you make professional decisions about your practice rather than feeling pressured into them.

Discussing previous adjustments in approaches to helping children learn to read will help you realise the extent to which developments have been professionally determined. Discussion with colleagues will also help the process of developing a whole-school approach. Positive growth is easier to sustain if decisions are taken collectively, with all parties aware of the background.

Think carefully about a development which has taken place in your school. Note it down.

How far did sources outside the school influence the way in which the development took place?

Were these influences helpful and positive or did they constrain?

Did the school anticipate the external influences?

In what ways did the school consciously manage to respond to these influences?

Were there any serious pressure points?

If we can identify the sources of external influence through looking back on previous experience, we can begin to realise the extent to which we are responding to the climate in which we all work.

Consider the catchment area of your school.

Jot down the three most important social factors which affect the school.

Compare your jottings with a colleague.

Look at the important issues that are emerging and try to work out how they influence the way in which you approach aspects of your work in teaching. It may be that you talk about reading but find yourself focusing on other aspects of curriculum.

Do the social factors encourage you to take new initiatives in the curriculum, or do they inhibit the sort of developments that are planned?

13

Chapter 2

HOW DO YOU
TEACH READING?
The teacher's perspective

The aim of this chapter is twofold. First, we want to enable you to reflect upon your own present practice in terms of how you approach reading in your classroom and school. Secondly, we want you to receive the benefit of other primary school teachers' ideas and views. In order to achieve this, we will pose questions designed to help you consider what you do every day with the children in your classes. These questions are taken from a questionnaire we sent out in 1987 to over 100 teachers in Cumbria and West London. Their answers and selected comments follow so that you will be able to compare your responses and consider their ideas. Some of these will simply confirm what you already do and believe, but others may well be surprising. In either case, reflection upon them and taking stock of present practice has to be the starting point for any future development.

Before looking at reading in detail, some general points can be made from our survey. These generalisations, in fact, confirm our own perceptions gained from spending a great deal of time in schools and working with teachers on in-service courses. Perhaps they are best summed up by one local authority adviser with responsibility for the early years of schooling. When asked for her perceptions of what was happening in the schools she visited, she replied:

I should like to stress that I do see real changes taking place. I am certain that schools are generally using a wider variety of books for the initial teaching of reading. There has been a growing movement towards taking books home and involving parents in reading in some way. Perhaps the most significant change over the recent past is the hearing of reading twice or so a week as opposed to every day.

Her perceptions are more interesting when seen in connection with the questionnaires. The teachers' replies clearly show that there is a tremendous diversity of practice with regard to the teaching of reading, and that many teachers are questioning their practice and beginning to implement changes. The present debate concerning approaches and materials has certainly affected teachers' perceptions of how best to work in the classroom and what is the place of parents in the process.

It is perhaps worrying that the great diversity of practice and perceptions is often to be found within the same school. It would appear that children moving up through many schools will encounter very different practice year by year, teacher by teacher. We can only wonder what they make of this and how it affects their progress and attitude towards reading. One illustration will suffice here. The responses in a large infant school to a question concerning what children did when they had finished a book show that some teachers allow free choice of the next 'reading book', others direct the children to the next book in the reading scheme and still others point children to books in a colour-coded (or other) system. In other words, the three choices we presented are all being followed by different teachers in the same school.

This chapter can be used by staff to build up some sort of picture of what exactly is happening in their school. This could form the basis of a school-wide consideration of present reading policy as a prelude to deciding on future developments. We would suggest that teachers work

15

through the questions in a group, although individuals on their own will also find it useful. Much will be gained by discussing the questions and your responses fully before looking at the survey results. Making each question a TIME OUT can be an effective way of using the survey.

The survey is presented in two parts. The first examines teachers' views about reading in the classroom, including materials, organisation and methods, and the second looks at teachers' perceptions of the part parents ought to play. An auxiliary section presents the perceptions of parents in the form of diaries kept over the course of some weeks by two mothers of reception children.

TEACHERS AND READING SURVEY

Q *For this question you are given a series of alternatives. Please choose only one of these alternatives.*
Teachers hold many different views about how best to help children learn to read. Do you think this is best effected by:

(a) children following a structured reading scheme?
(b) children using a selection of graded or coded reading materials?
(c) children using books from a selection of different schemes?
(d) children following a teacher-directed scheme with the additional option of reading other books of their own choice?
(e) children having a free choice of individual titles using non-reading scheme books?

If you are working with colleagues, discuss your choice and the reasons for it.

A The percentage of teachers choosing each of the alternatives was:

(a) 7%   (b) 24%   (c) 20%   (d) 28%   (e)21%

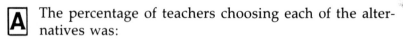

« *I am beginning to introduce an individualised approach to reading in the classroom.*

To keep track of individual progress it is necessary to have a disciplined approach to a school's reading scheme.

From 40 years' experience with every type of age group and ability — [I'd say you need] reading scheme + look and say + phonetics.

I have not tried teaching beginners without a 'scheme' — I would want to prove for myself that this worked. Would try it.

I find the need to follow a more structured scheme with the very young children until they have acquired a basic vocabulary.

Books and courses I have attended over the past six months have influenced me to re-think my approach to the teaching of reading. I am now particularly interested in the role that 'real books' have to play in the development of readers. **»**

Q Have you noticed any changes within the last two years in the kinds of books purchased in your school for children learning to read?

A Only 5% of teachers answered no to this question. All of the teachers who answered yes were using a wider variety of books characterised by a number of features which appeared again and again. These characteristics are represented in their comments.

« *When I first came to this school three years ago, the main scheme was* Through the rainbow *with some* One, two, three and away *books. In the last three years there has been a great change. There are now lots of interesting and lively non-reading scheme books available plus* Story chest *books, some* Ginn 360 *books, dual-text books and* Terrace house *books. The range of materials available is much more extensive and interesting. Teaching reading is much more fun and I would imagine it must be for the children too!*

A current issue in our school. As yet we have not changed the one basic reading scheme but are bringing in other schemes and books alongside.

There has been a move away from reading scheme books and much more emphasis has been placed on storybooks and picture books.

More dual-text books, storybooks by popular authors and books without text (pictures only). Less of the reading scheme series. More paperbacks. More multi-ethnic books are in evidence. A more careful approach to books in general — sexist and racist books have been weeded out of old stock and dumped! Replacement books 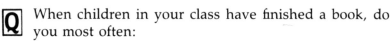 *have been carefully studied.*

Q When children in your class have finished a book, do you most often:

(a) direct them to the next book in the reading scheme?
(b) allow them to choose within a colour-coded (or other) system?
(c) allow them to choose freely from any books in the classroom?

A Responses to this question were split almost equally:

(a) 34%   (b) 35%   (c) 31%

I don't let children choose until they have reached a certain level and have a vocabulary of 30+ words (reading the words).

At the end of J4 I allow them to choose freely from a selected range of paperbacks.

I work on the premise that children will be more likely to succeed in reading the books they choose for themselves.

We use many schemes but I pick the next book.

If the book is from the class library they are free to choose any book they wish. If it is one from the reading scheme then they may select one from their particular group.

We use the A–Z system of grading books. So children may choose any book on their level (eg choose any book from level F).

Q It is typical Monday morning. By the end of Friday would you be aiming to have:

(a) heard every child in your class read to you more than once?
(b) heard every child in your class read to you once?
(c) heard some children read as part of your programme of hearing each child regularly?
(d) heard some children only if and when you have time?
(e) spent time in ways which do not include listening to children read?

A The teachers in our survey chose in the following way:

(a) 49%   (b) 22%   (c) 23%   (d) 2%   (e) 4%

« *Those children with special reading difficulties will obviously be heard more than once.*

By the phrase 'heard child read' I mean sharing a reading experience. This may mean the child reading to me or with me or myself reading to the child.

Children read to themselves and to each other as part of the programme.

Reading from books chosen is only part of learning to read.

I think it's important to share books with children — on a one-to-one basis. Although every child may not actually have read to me — I would aim to have spent time sharing a book or talking about a book with each child more than once a week. I like to do **»** *this in the book corner.*

Q In a typical week do you hope to read aloud to the class:

(a) more than once a week?
(b) once a day?
(c) two or three times a week?
(d) if and when you have time?

A Teachers in our survey chose the following responses:

(a) 30%   (b) 36%   (c) 27%   (d) 7%

19

« *I believe every child should be read to EVERY DAY of their WHOLE school life.*

I enjoy it and so do they — it's an excellent opportunity for developing listening skills, language skills and also reading skills— quite apart from sharing the enjoyment of a good story.

All types of reading to children are vital, eg poems, rhymes, songs.

I feel the sharing of good stories with the class is time well spent and we refer to stories read all the time during class conversations.

When I've completed a book with a class I allow children to borrow it. By the end of the year a dozen or so books will be circulating and most children will have borrowed three or four. »

Q *This question offers you a series of alternatives. You may choose more than one of these alternatives.*
When you give time to an individual child, do you:

(a) ask the child to read aloud to you while you listen?
(b) encourage the child to talk about the book rather than read it aloud?
(c) join in and read alongside the child?

A The number of times a particular option was chosen by the teachers in our survey was:

(a) 79   (b) 70   (c) 56

« *Each child necessitates a different approach. Competent readers — (a) and (b); poorer readers — (c); (b) is an excellent method employed when children are keen readers and take their books home to check they have read sections at home.*

When a child becomes a fluent reader I do not consider it necessary to hear them read a whole book. The child chooses the story they liked best to read to me and discuss the other stories.

Usually (a) and (b) at any one session, (c) if child struggling a little or reading to speed up.

Really a combination of (a), (b), (c). Talking about the book is ESSENTIAL — AND THE CHILD WANTS TO READ TO YOU — PLUS PAIRED READING AS NEEDED.

I ask questions about the book and on vocabulary etc.

I begin by reading alongside the child and find that usually the child reaches a stage where they want to break away and show how well they can read to you by themselves. **»**

5 minutes

Q ***This question offers you a series of alternatives. You may choose more than one of these alternatives.***
You are listening to a child reading and you find the child stops at a particular word. Do you:

(a)   encourage the child to sound out the word?
(b)   pause for a few seconds and then tell the child?
(c)   supply the word immediately?
(d)   talk about the context?
(e)   let the child miss the word out?
(f) encourage the child to look at the picture?
(g)   encourage the child to guess?

A The number of times a particular option was chosen by the teachers in our survey was:

(a) 67   (b) 61   (c) 20   (d) 71   (e) 3   (f) 66   (g) 59

« *I aim to keep the flow of the story going and would attempt to supply the word quickly.*

I use a mixture of phonics (if the word is phonetically spelled) and clues from the story.

First is sounding out. If the child cannot do so then I give the word. I would encourage using the picture to guess.

All these are strategies which I use — (a) is the one I will only use if I feel it is relevant for the child in question. Would prefer to let the child use a variety of strategies involving phonics, context, pictures rather than sounding out which can be frustrating and not relevant.

I encourage the child to look at the word more carefully, the initial letter especially, and have a go. After a few seconds I supply the word.

All of these — the only sounding out is probably of initial letter or blend and perhaps the ending where appropriate.

I encourage the child to miss the word, read on and then guess from context. I always give words which I know are not within their experience or understanding and discuss the meaning.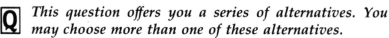

Q ***This question offers you a series of alternatives. You may choose more than one of these alternatives.***
Over the years there has been much discussion about the involvement of parents in children's reading. Which of these types of parental involvement is closest to the practice in your classroom?

(a) Parents are not involved and books do not go home.
(b) Children are encouraged to choose books to take home to read with parents.
(c) Children are given a book by you to take home to read to parents.
(d) Parents work in the classroom with children.
(e) You have an organised system of home-school reading programmes, including guidance and recorded correspondence.

A The number of times a particular option was chosen by the teachers in our survey was:

(a) 7   (b) 68   (c) 46   (d) 23   (e) 30

« *Parents rarely offer to work in classroom due to other commitments, eg work.*

Parents now working successfully in classes.

Children are allowed to take home any books that they are interested in from the school library. Ginn 360 *is not taken home.*

Parents have been approached but there has not been much response.

Home-school links include parents in groups of six to see me at each stage of the reading programme, ie to practise and explain paired reading.

I have a group of mothers who hear my strongest readers each week, freeing me for the weaker ones.

Q *This question offers you a series of alternatives. You may choose more than one of these alternatives.*
Over the recent years there has been much discussion about the involvement of parents in children's reading. Do you consider:

(a) teaching children to read should be left to teachers?
(b) the best way to involve parents is by allowing children to take books home?
(c) parents have a significant role to play in the classroom?
(d) the most benefit can come from a teacher-directed programme for parents and children to read together at home?
(e) the best way for children to learn is from their parents at home, with the teacher in a supporting role?
(f) the best way for children to learn to read is for their parents to teach them?

A The number of times a particular option was chosen by the teachers in our survey was:

(a) 19   (b) 6   (c) 55   (d) 65   (e) 17   (f) 8

« *Parents are the best asset we have and we must have the conviction of our ideals and use them.*

Teaching reading is a skill — not all parents have either the training or the skill.

Children start their reading at home listening to stories — our methods should be a continuation of that, not in opposition to it. We can best develop their reading skills and enjoyment by working together.

Parents and teachers should work together in partnership.

I'm sure parents have a lot to offer but quite how we tap this source I don't know. Many appear to be very reluctant. Contact is very important.

As a parent of young children myself it is difficult to separate my roles at times! I know as a parent I want to be involved in my children's learning — it gives me enormous satisfaction to be involved and know what they have been doing in class. Children are learning all the time — I would like to think that we are all supporting each other in helping the children to make sense of their world. »

If the above questions and responses are used by schools at in-service meetings, we believe they offer an excellent starting point for a consideration of the teaching and learning of reading. The last two questions are concerned with teachers' perspectives of the involvement of parents. But parents should have their voice heard as well.

In order to gauge how her parents were reacting to being formally involved with their children's reading, Carol Green, a reception class teacher at St George's primary school, Barrow-in-Furness, asked some of them to keep a record of what was happening at home, while she herself kept a journal. Two of the parents' reports make fascinating reading. One is extremely positive, the sort we might hope for from involved parents. The other vividly points up some of the problems. It is worth asking how we would react to these parents if their children were in our own classes. We believe without doubt that parents should be involved in their children's reading, and that we must face up to the challenge of the first report. Perhaps the strongest argument is that most parents will become involved one way or another, so we must ensure that home and school are working together.

Parent One

When N started school I was very worried because she is very stubborn and I thought she would never settle down and learn anything, but once she started bringing books home she started having the confidence to learn. But she always needs reassuring that she is doing everything just right. When N started bringing her books home she would not read the right words; she started getting angry. That made me angry too so we would give up till the next day. Then one day I went to school and Mrs Green showed me that she had been holding N's fingers on hers and learning each word individually and that really helped her a lot. But she still would only read when she wanted to. Over the months, though, she comes home and wants to sit and learn, pointing to each different word; but she's been finding it hard to remember words. She can start reading the beginning of the book; then, as she gets half way, she can't remember the words. But she has been really excited because now she reads them with hardly any help from me.

Today went to pick up N from school. She told me that Mrs Green had changed to letting the children pick their own books. It was all right at first; then she would just bring them home and just put them on the shelf and not bother with them. She would read her sisters' books but when it came to her own she just started having her tantrums and get me so mad I would throw the book and say "Well, you will never learn."

Today N was just sitting on the chair at home pretending to be reading the book by making the story up. Later on when I came back in the room she was with her dad, reading the book that she wouldn't read to me. Then after she had read it to her dad she came and read some of it to me, then got tired so we gave up for the night. But we both praised her on how well she had read it and she went to bed with a big smile on her face. The only book I have found that she won't read is the ABC book. She likes to tell me the alphabet but when it came to the word to go with the letter she just wouldn't even try; but her books that she brings home at the moment are the read-it-yourself ones. She reads them quite well but tends to look at the pictures instead of the words even though she's pointing to the word.

Today N came home with *Sleeping beauty* and she really liked the book so she read it twice to me and once to her dad.

6.5.87 Today N brought a book called *Meg on the moon*. She will not read it either to me or her dad. She says we can't read it properly. She finds it hard getting back into the routine of reading when they have the holidays.

14.5.87 N brought a book home and said that she couldn't read it, so I sat patiently trying to help her read it, but she still wouldn't so I put it away and later in the evening she read the whole thing through to her dad.

19.5.87 Today N was stubborn at first, then later on she said, "Come on mam, let's try and read the book." But she had picked one that had lots of sentences; she tried really hard to get every word right but she couldn't — only the ones she already knows.

2.6.87 Today N brought a book but she said she would not even try to read it, but later on she gave it a try but started moaning so I stopped reading with her. The next morning she got up and started reading the whole book to M with no bother.

16.6.87 We are back at square one again. N said she won't even try to read her book. She gets like this when she has a holiday so I leave her and she gets back to the routine. But my own opinion is that the children shouldn't pick their own books because N, for example, brings most of the books with hard words on purpose knowing she can't read them and won't even try; but maybe if we wait a little longer she might just pick the right book to suit her.

Parent Two

As adults, we take reading very much for granted. I only realised this when it came to J learning to read. I would never have tried to teach J to read at a pre-school age, for fear of confusing him later on. Anyway, I would have felt as if I was forcing him.

J has always had books around him at home and has always loved them, even as a baby. So I felt quite confident that he would soon settle down to reading when he started school.

At first, I was a bit unsure of the reading method at St George's. All I knew was that some schools used the reading tin method, which didn't seem to be in operation at my son's school.

However, his teacher soon explained everything to me and I felt much better, although I still couldn't see any set pattern of reading until I actually went into the classroom and read with some pupils myself. I enjoyed this very much, although I half expected the other children to read in the exact way as J does! One little girl said every word correct while looking at me, not the book. She obviously knew that story very well! It reminded me that children only learn from memory.

At the present moment in time I am very pleased with J's school progress in general. It makes it so much better for me and his dad to see how much he enjoys his reading. Learning should be fun.

Like most mums I probably expected a little too much too soon when J first started school. Especially with him being our first child, it was all so new to me as well.

I'm quite happy now to see him going at his own steady pace. I never say, "Right - we'll read this now." I just wait for him to come to me (or dad) as that's obviously just when he wants to. And he never disappoints me – but I wouldn't tell him if he had!

Favourite books:

Puddle Lane   Easy-to-read, colourful, interesting and short versions of the story for a child to read.

Meg and Mog   I don't like these books. I don't find them readable at all but J finds them very funny.

Mr Men   J and his little brother love to giggle at these. Ideal for younger children, I think.

Push and pull   Black and white, but very informative – gives J something to think about. He brings it home quite often.

Inside outside upside down   This one he can read himself with no bother because it is so repetitive, yet still interesting. It is so easy to learn. J soon got to know the shapes of the letters.

Mrs Wobble the waitress   I like this book myself as it is not too boring. Simple and repetitive. Nicely illustrated too, which counts for a lot.

Over in the meadow   A counting rhyme book. J likes this because he can read it all the way through.

Doing the washing   I like the drawings in this one. They give lots of openings for talking about other things. Not too wordy.

Chapter 3

THE CHILD
Skills and perceptions

The last chapter looked at the teaching of reading through the eyes of the adults involved, teachers and parents. We now want to switch the focus and examine reading in terms of the children themselves. This will be done in two ways. First, we will consider what children of four and five bring with them to school in the way of skills and awareness which teachers could, and indeed, should, make use of in their teaching strategies. Reception children are not blank slates, ignorant of stories, books and reading. They have much on which we can build.

Secondly, we report the views of nearly 200 children, mainly juniors but with some infants, who were asked to answer a questionnaire. We have not attempted any detailed analysis of their replies, but simply ask you to consider the selection we offer. What does it tell us about their thoughts and feelings concerning their developing reading ability?

WHAT CHILDREN BRING WITH THEM TO SCHOOL

Five years of pre-school learning In order to sort out approaches to reading with young children, some consideration ought to be given to the skills and knowledge four- and five-year-olds already have when they enter school. Teaching is about moving children on from what they already know and can do. That such a consideration should form the rationale behind our teaching strategies will probably seem obvious, yet it has in fact been neglected in the past. The teaching of reading has only recently recognised the value of harnessing the ability and understanding children have acquired even at an early age.

They can talk! Every normal five-year-old child has learned to talk — has mastered the mother tongue. This happens so naturally that there is a danger we won't realise what a tremendous achievement it represents. Yet talking is crucial to success at reading, both in terms of what children have learned and how they have gone about learning it.

Words and how we put them together Pre-school children amass a vocabulary of thousands of words, and internalise the grammar in order to understand the speech of others and to form their own sentences. Not bad without a day spent in school! The acquisition of a vocabulary is what most people see as language development. It is a staggering enough achievement in its own right. The learning of something as abstract and complex as grammar may well appear impossible but pre-school children manage it. Just spend some time talking freely to a three-, four- or five-year-old. Listen carefully to what they say and pay particular attention to the mistakes they make. You will soon realise what they have learned. For example, a child runs up to his father and shouts, "Dad, I runned up the hill!" Or another child explains that Goldilocks has "aten" her porridge. In both of these examples, the children are using a version of the past tense. In applying the rule for

30

forming the past tense, they have made mistakes, but they are certainly aware of the rules. As soon as children put words in the right order, they are using basic grammar correctly.

Such knowledge is vitally important for reading. We use our grammatical awareness to help us through the sentences on the page. Consider a sentence beginning: "She walked into the..."

In terms of English grammar, only certain classes of words can now follow — a noun (room, hall, garden) or an adjective (big, dark, wide). We know that a pronoun would result in nonsense: "She walked into the she/he/it/them."

This grammatical knowledge is different from our general knowledge which tells us that she is more likely to walk into a room or a hall than a sausage or a worm, which is also grammatically correct. We use both types of knowledge to make our way through the words on the page because we expect the passage we are reading to make sense. Uppermost in our minds as we read is the meaning of what we are reading. We simply use the words to get this meaning.

When approaches to reading are discussed below, these points should make us consider carefully:

> The sorts of text we should give young children if we want them to use all they know about their language from the start.

How do they do it? The errors in speaking made by young children also indicate how they go about learning their language. This has great implications for reading. The first point to make is that they have not been sitting about waiting passively for someone to teach them how to talk. Parents do not actually give their children talking lessons. But if nobody formally teaches them, how do they accomplish it? At the root of all their learning is the fact that children have a strong drive to make sense of their world, and language has a vital role to play in this. Rather than being taught to speak, children actively learn.

All that appears to be necessary for children to achieve this learning successfully is to grow up in an environment in which people are talking, and to be able to join in. From the start, their parents provide just such an environment. Not only is conversation a feature of every home, but parents talk to their children long before they can possibly make sense of what is being said to them. However, parents do not engage in all this talk in order to teach speech. They do so because they want to communicate with their children. They want to share the events and feelings which make up their lives. Family life provides rich experiences, and parents and children talk about them. Words and grammatical constructions are used in a natural way, and slowly but surely children begin to use them too.

At a very simple level, imitation is involved — parents pointing to things, naming them and children repeating. But the errors of past tense mentioned above show us that something much more subtle is going on. The child who comes out with "runned" cannot be imitating an adult, who would say "ran". What has happened is that the child has heard a number of past tenses ending in "ed" and decides to apply the rule to the verb run. Eventually children learn to use "ran", realising that their original attempt was incorrect. Often such learning occurs because parents provide the correct word or expression in response. So the father of this particular child might comment, "Oh, so you ran up the hill, did you?" The fact that the child has made a mistake is accepted by the parent; no-one expects word-perfect speech from the start. Similarly children feel free to make mistakes. Because their attention is focused on what they are trying to say, they will use language in the best way they can in order to say it. What parents do not do is sit children down for a lesson on English past tenses. That would be enough to put an end to all conversation. The aim of both parent and child is communication — the use of language to share experiences. So language is learned almost unconsciously.

Children, then, learn their mother tongue for themselves. Adults, through the environment they provide and their conversations with their children, make this learning possible. In his book *The meaning makers*, Gordon Wells describes this process and provides many fascinating examples. Underlying the learning is the basic desire of children to join in all of the talk that is going on around

see ref. 3

them. They want to be a part of everything. They begin to use language for themselves because of what it enables them to do — to say that they want something, to express feelings, to explain something that has happened. Michael Halliday *see ref. 4* has called this 'learning how to mean' and Frank Smith the 'I want another cream bun' theory of language development. Always the attention is on the meaning of what is being said: that is what motivates children to learn how to talk.

When considering approaches to reading, the ways in which children learn to talk should lead to a consideration of:

> The sort of environment which will best motivate and enable children to learn to read.
>
> How to focus their attention on the meaning of what they are reading rather than on the language in which it is written.
>
> Our attitude to the mistakes they will inevitably make.

THE MEANING OF PRINT

Growing up in this country, children are surrounded by print. In other words, they are surrounded by reading. From

their earliest days they will look at the peculiar squiggles around them, on television, shop fronts, packets, tins, newspapers, magazines. As they grow older, they will notice their parents and others looking at these marks and making meaning out of them. They will ask, "What's it say?" and learn to recognise Tesco or Marks and Spencer, Warrington or St Andrews, depending on where they live and the shops they are taken to. When they ask, their parents will obviously answer their questions. This means that, by the time they arrive at school, all children know something about print and reading. They expect it to make sense — to have some meaning. They must surely expect that it will continue to do so in the classroom. Some will already have learned to read. All will want to become readers for, as Frank Smith puts it, they will want to join 'The Literacy Club'. They will have definite expectations concerning reading and learning to read at school.

In terms of our role in helping them learn to read, we need to consider:

> How we can reflect in our classrooms the print environment in which children grow up.
>
> What sort of written material will make sense to a young child.
>
> How we can encourage children to continue to ask questions about reading.

ONCE UPON A TIME...THE POWER OF STORY

It has been said that children learn to read in order to read stories. While the print environment described above must certainly act as a vital force in motivating children to read, stories and storybooks are special. It is difficult to analyse why a good story should cast such a spell on a reader or listener, but we all recognise that it does. A teacher reading a story knows exactly when the magic is taking effect. The eyes of the children take on a faraway look, mouths drop open, all goes quiet. An intense atmosphere builds up in the room. This just does not happen in maths or spelling or PE, no matter how interesting they are. We realise at these moments that we are dealing with something very special. Surely we should harness this power in our work with young readers.

Children who have grown up in homes where story has been a regular feature of their lives will already be hooked by the time they get to school. They will already have built up a repertoire of stories which they know and love. Now they want to learn to read them for themselves. In addition to this powerful motivation, they will also have developed some impressive skills and knowledge which should, if recognised and used by the teacher, help them become readers. In order to demonstrate these, simply ask any four- or five-year-old to tell a story they know well. Listen out for evidence of the following:

language Children who have listened to lots of stories develop an awareness of the differences between written language and oral language. They could not explain these, but they demonstrate their awareness through their own storytelling. First, stories are told in the past tense; secondly, and more subtly, written language has a rhythm of its own. We can tell very quickly whether or not someone is reading or talking just by listening to the rhythm of the language. Children seem to internalise this awareness of rhythm and use it unconsciously when telling a story.

structure All stories have a beginning, a middle, and an end: from conventional openings, such as 'Once upon a time', through the adventures of the characters to conventional endings, such as '... and they all lived happily every after'. Again children build up an awareness of the way stories are put together. Those with access to a rich variety of picture storybooks build up quite a sophisticated awareness of how stories can be told.

Story characters Children's stories, like adult fiction, contain characters. These are stock figures in traditional folk and fairy tales: witches, fairy godmothers, stepmothers and stepfathers, animals. Of course, children often have the most important role in a story.

Dramatic events A good story is a series of dramatic events. A successful storyteller therefore tells the story dramatically. The voice is used with varying intonation, pace and volume in order to convey the drama of the tale to the listener. A child telling the story of Goldilocks will use a deep voice for Daddy Bear, a high one for Mummy Bear and a babyish squeak for Baby Bear.

The dramatic use of the voice shows that the focus of attention is on the story being told or read. Of course, the story must be a good one to prompt the use of the voice in this way.

STORIES AND THINKING

Most children arrive at school having experienced the power of stories and knowing a great deal about the way they are constructed and the language in which they are written. This would appear to be a solid base on which to build their progress as readers. Story seems to be one of the fundamental factors in the process of children becoming literate.

The research undertaken by Gordon Wells in Bristol followed the development of children who were one-year-olds when the research began. These children progressed at different rates in learning to read and write. Those who learned to read most rapidly and easily at school had been exposed to lots of stories in the years before school. Some of the reasons for this have been discussed above, but Wells suggests that something else might also be happening. Nearly all of the early intellectual development of children occurs in situations at home that are 'context-bound'. That is, the talking and thinking are about objects and events which are present at the time: birds in the garden, toys in a shop window, meals being prepared, clothes being washed. But sharing a story means thinking in a different way. The events being described are not happening there in the room; the child has to think outside the immediate context and find the language to express these thoughts.

see ref. 5 This is what Margaret Donaldson has called 'disembedded thought', the ability to think outside an immediate context which is vital for learning at school. It would appear, then, that story is much more than just a pleasurable activity

36

tagged on to the end of a day and not as important as other more 'school-like' work. It is fundamental for the development of thought and language. Children who have not experienced stories at home are likely to find learning to read and write difficult. This was true of one little girl in the Wells research, who seems never to have read a story before she arrived at school. Story is central to the development of literacy.

When thinking about early reading in school we must:

> Use stories as a prime motivating force for children.
>
> Allow and encourage children to use the skills and knowledge they possess concerning stories and the language of writing.

In this chapter we have argued that children arrive at school knowing a great deal about their language, both in its spoken and written forms. They are not blank slates on which, at the age of five, teachers can start to write. It would seem obvious to make use of what children bring with them to school if we want to make learning to read meaningful, and therefore easy. An awareness on our part of their skills and knowledge leads inevitably towards certain teaching strategies. These are based on viewing reading through the eyes of children.

WHAT HAPPENS WHEN WE READ STORIES?

We have argued that story should play a key part in the early reading of young children. It would seem to follow that the books we provide as early readers should be storybooks. We will certainly argue this below. Continuing the theme of examining reading from the child's perspective, we now must look at reading itself. What exactly happens when a reader sits down with a story or a novel?

Consider the following statement:

> Reading involves an interaction between a reader and a text.

As fluent adult readers, we would all recognise a reader and a text as the two sides to the reading equation, and that reading is an interaction. The use of the word 'interaction' implies that reading is a two-way process. Certainly the text brings its meaning to the reader, but of equal importance is the way the reader brings meaning to the text. We could show it like this:

> READER→ → →INTERACTION← ← ←TEXT

As the words on the page are read, there will be general agreement among different readers as to their meaning. This is what the text brings to the reader. But what about the meanings different readers bring to the text? Or, to put it another way, why do readers respond differently to the same writing? The text does not change, but the responses of the readers — and even professional critics — will often vary considerably. If any group of people are asked to rate the same story or poem on a scale from 'superb' to 'dreadful', we would be extremely surprised if they all agreed. They have brought different expectations, skills, knowledge, opinions, beliefs, personalities and life experiences to the reading. With each of these factors contributing to how we read, *see ref. 6* no wonder we respond differently. As Fred Inglis has written about how we respond to characters in novels: "We respond in complex ways, to and for them out of the framework of all our prior experiences."

Whatever we read, our attention is on the meaning of the words rather than the words or letters themselves. When we read stories or novels we are taken up with the characters and what is happening to them. The words on the page become pictures in the reader's mind and these pictures will be very personal. To test this, just close your eyes and think of a novel you have read. A description of a second world war battlefield will trigger different pictures in the minds of an ex-soldier and a 20-year-old. Whatever the words say, the soldier's pictures will owe a great deal to his memories. We realise how important these pictures are whenever a film or television version is made of a novel we have read. The characters and places never look the same as we imagined them to be.

This discussion of the subjective way in which readers read — the importance the reader plays in the reading process — has been neglected in the past with regard to the teaching of reading. Many of the methods advocated and the materials written have taken little or no account of how and why readers read. Yet it is vitally important because all readers, be they four years old or 40 years old, interact with and respond to what they read in the same ways. They make connections between themselves and their lives and what they read. Examples from children make the point dramatically: Helen, 11 years old, on the mother in Nina Bawden's *The peppermint pig* — "I thought of my mum...she's always telling me off...but it's good for me really." Gavin, 11 years old, on Tom in Philippa Pearce's *Tom's midnight garden* — "He doesn't like his Aunt Gwen because she's a child lover and he don't like people like them. He don't like people who go on at you and things like that and bothering too much about you, saying you can't do things like that." Jenny, four years old, knew the story of Goldilocks off by heart and 'read' it aloud. Every so often she would break off to comment on what was happening: "Goldilocks, you know, she's very hungry because, you see, she hasn't eaten any breakfast." When Goldilocks broke Baby Bear's chair, Jenny said: "That's because she's too big. Perhaps she's seven or eight ...Well I think she'd be all right if she was one or two."

see ref. 7

see ref. 8

Reading or listening to a story at any age is entering a magical world created by an author, into which we take ourselves and our lives. Our attention is on what is happening in that world. The words on the page simply enable us to get there. Reading is not about getting the words right. It is about getting behind the words to the meaning. If this is what fluent readers do, we need to consider how best to help learner readers do the same.

The issues examined above will now be used to examine briefly some of the arguments surrounding the teaching of reading today. In doing so, we point the way towards the sort of classroom organisation, home-school links and teaching strategies which we advocate later in the book.

WHAT SHOULD CHILDREN READ?
MATERIALS AND METHODS

This part of the reading process — what is being read — has been the focus of attention of teachers, reading experts and publishers for many years. There has been a search for the best way of simplifying the English language so as to make reading easier for children. The attempts have been many and varied, and have given rise to different approaches to the teaching of reading. One method, still current, has children learning letters and words before progressing to sentences and finally to a book. The argument is that books, and the sentences in them, are more complicated than words and letters. Therefore, children cannot possibly attempt a book until they have a 'slight vocabulary' of a number of words. Books based on this method are written with a view to introducing new words in a controlled way, so that children are able to build up their reading vocabulary under controlled conditions. The books must therefore be read in the right order.

Another method is concerned with the complexity of the sound-symbol relationships in the English language. The argument is that the key to reading success lies in the child's ability to turn into sounds the letters and groups of letters which make up words. By blending these sounds together, words can be read. Books specially written for this phonic method introduce sound-symbol relationships in a graded and controlled way, with plenty of repetition to assist learning: "Will hid a pill in his till".

Such specially written materials and methods not only fail to take account of the skills, knowledge and motivation possessed by children, but actually prevent making use of them. For instance, the language bears no relationship to English as it is used normally, so children's awareness of grammar in terms of predicting the sorts of words likely to occur at a particular point in a sentence is of little help. Worse is the content of so many such books. Because the emphasis is on getting the language right, little consideration is given to the quality of the subject matter. A child who has grown up on a rich diet of folk and fairy tales, together with many powerful modern picture books and stories, is faced with an anaemic world in the specially written reading book. Instead of entering the magical world of story and being caught up in exciting and dramatic events, the child's attention is focused firmly on the words on the page and the need simply to read them correctly.

In the last few years, great efforts have been made by some publishers to improve the quality of the books which make up their reading schemes, though most remain feeble when compared to non-reading scheme books. The publishers try hard to justify their wares in terms of 'modern approaches'. A glance at the advertisement language of some of them shows this: 'variety and choice', 'real stories and whole language', 'plan...reading development realistically, comprehensively and effectively'. Some of this is just the meaningless language of advertising, but it is of concern because of the use of such language for packages which still place books in some mythical order depending on the complexity of the writing, as if learning to read followed a linear route represented by such a scheme. The issues examined above show what a naive and simplistic view this is of language development. No matter how colourful and lively the books, once they are numbered or coloured and placed in order,

and children are allowed to read them only in that order, they force teachers, parents and children into thinking and behaving in accordance with this particular view of reading. In the minds of children, reading becomes concerned with getting on to the next book, getting a more difficult book, getting through the scheme. Parents worry if their children bring 'easy' books home. Teachers try to match children with books that are 'just right' — which seems to mean not too difficult but difficult enough to make a child struggle a little. How many of us would read the newspapers if they were 'just right' for us? The emphasis remains firmly on the ability of children to decode the words on the page.

TEACHING READING OR LEARNING TO READ?

While arguments continue to rage about the best methods of teaching reading, and publishers vie with each other to meet or create demand, the vast majority of children quietly go on learning to read. It is often said that this shows any method and materials will work, but in fact it shows that children take on the business of learning to read for themselves. They use their skills, knowledge and tremendous motivation to make sense of reading, just as they have already made sense of talking.

Teachers teach and children learn, but we must be wary of assuming too great a connection between the two. Children who are given their few minutes of reading aloud to the teacher every day learn to read but could they really learn on just a few minutes a day? Would they learn to talk if they were only allowed to talk for a few minutes a day? Perhaps only those who fail to make progress initially go searching among the teaching strategies employed in their classrooms for the key to success.

If children are in fact learning to read in much the same way they learn to talk, our attention should be on how these are related. The following two suggestions on what reading material should be provided should therefore come as no surprise:

- Storybooks of all shapes and sizes from which children can choose on their own.

- Materials around the classroom which reflect the literate environment they are growing up in — posters, signs, instructions to be followed, reminders to be referred to, letters to be read, for example.

A classroom containing such books and materials will be providing great motivation for children to learn to read — partly by creating in them a need to read. What is the teacher's role in this?

HOW DO WE HELP? READING BOOKS

What exactly happens within the sort of environment suggested above is very simple. With regard to their reading books, children choose from those on display in the classroom and share them with others — the teacher, parents, any other adult helping in the school. Older children can also spend time reading with the younger ones each week.

What happens in a reading session will vary: sometimes the child will simply listen to the book being read aloud; sometimes the child and adult will read in unison; sometimes the child will read certain bits; sometimes the child will take the lead and read, with help provided where and when necessary. Always there should be encouragement for the child to stop the reading and comment on what has happened or may be about to happen; to laugh, share excitement, explore the illustrations. Children will read some books a number of times before leaving them, sharing them with different people at school and at home. There is always the chance to re-read an old favourite. Slowly but surely the marks on the page become recognisable as words, for the same words occur over and over again in storybooks. They take on meaning through the telling of the stories.

A teacher's role is not only to be a part of this process, but to organise and advise the other helpers, especially parents who are working with their children at home. To try to do the whole thing on your own with 30 infants is well nigh impossible, and leads inevitably to the sort of structured approach represented by reading schemes. Perhaps it is the teachers rather than the children who need these schemes. Parents are a resource with a vested interest in the progress of their children. Making use of them and others leaves you freer to emphasise the power of what is being read, and the delight which comes from sharing it.

'URGENT READING' IN THE CLASSROOM

The second side to reading, an environment that reflects the reading which surrounds children at home and in the street, is equally simple. The major requirement is reading with an immediate purpose, and the list of possibilities for such reading is endless. The only other requirements are active encouragement of children to ask about what they want to read, and help when they are reading it. Their natural curiosity and desire to make sense of their surroundings must be encouraged at school, just as it has been at home for *see ref. 9* the previous five years. Margaret Peters has written about 'urgent writing' and gives a lovely example of a teacher who encouraged parents to allow their children to write their absence notes, and to help them do it. Similarly, 'urgent reading', such as signs and notes, should surely be a feature of our classrooms.

CHILDREN'S VIEWS OF READING

On the next few pages we have selected some of the more thought-provoking, and frequently amusing, comments of children who were asked to fill in a questionnaire about reading. Most of the questions we asked are included, and we would suggest that you might like to use them with your own children. Trying to discover what children think and feel can only result in more sensitive, thoughtful teaching. We do not offer any comments on their responses, but they certainly should spark an interesting debate if discussed by staff. Perhaps the key question we need to ask about the children's comments is: what do these children think reading and learning to read is all about?

Think about all the reading you have done at home and in school. Which kind of reading do you enjoy most?

I enJoy reading comics the most

ghost stories.
adult.
adult stories.
and love storys.

Reading annualls

I enjoy reading most horror stories.

Funny books
at home (In bed)

I like books on noture and
Ghost Storys.

① Adventurs ② Finding out ③ Story books ④ Poems.
⑤ ① Womans own. Skary books 2nd best

I Don't enjoy reading

When you choose a new book, what is it that makes you pick it out?

the cover, the title, Sometimes I have read another berok by the same author that was good so I read the book, the information on the back.

Probebly the thikness of the book.

the cover picture, name, and the bit of writing on the back.

Think about the books you have read. What made them good?

the   things   that   made me
                    laugh

The big words and I like all of the adventures and it was call the fameus seven

They make you forget what else you should be doing.

They hold you in another world.   the teacher

wonling to no wot hapens next

Are there times when you find reading boring? When are they?

yes when i've been to told to stay in and i coudl Be out praying Football.

Somm some times when the teachers chose a book for me

When I chooose a libary book and and I don't like it and I have to read it beacause I have to do a beok Review.

yes on sunday   I hate   When I
                            reading   have to
                                          read them
                                          to miss

i dontit like reading when icome into school in the Morning

When I read it twice.

What do you find the hardest thing about reading?

breaking words down

It is harder for me to read aloud

I don't find eney think hard
bat when read in a group

Getting into a book
at the start

the hard writing

Puntuation

Boring books.

I think it is the small print I find
the hardest

uninteresting books like Animal Stories. I don't
like Water ship Down because it gives
me nightmares

In what ways has your reading improved?

my readings Impraved
when I go hewme and
sit by the fire

Reading some of the thesaurus has taught me some
weird words

up in the colours

Reading faster than I did.

by getting harder
books.

When the words
get Litter

What can your teachers do to help you read better?

me reuchers help you read better
because if you get words wrong
they help you like Paleontologists
I needed it to be broken up like
this PAI/E/on/TOL/o/gists.

Leave me alone

They help you on hard words

They can give us different sorts of books
that is easier for us to read.

They help me break up words.
(and find my place.)

by teaching you different
sorts of hard words

Is there anyone special you like to read to?

my brother matthew   I like to read to my Gran

I don't normally like to someone   but I think
its   my Dad, because he always lets me
correct words myself.
I would like reading to infants, but I don't
like reading to teachers.
My Mum.   My toy E.T.
I like reading to my cat
bers, my dog

48

When you are going to read a new book, what sort of things do you do before you start? Do you, perhaps, look at the pictures or talk about it with a friend?

I sit comfey and read

I look at the colour code on it and I look at the words to see if they are to hard or to easy.

look at the words to make sure they are not to hard

To start off with, with a new book I always look at the end three words.

look at the pictures

Do you like someone to read to you?

Yes, if it is a book I find hard to read

yes my mum

I like my sister to read to me.

yes_no aspesely when the theacher read it to us

yes my dad   yes my brother. Some of the time.

49

TIME OUT

1 hour

Look again at the responses of the children to the reading questionnaire.

Discuss with colleagues any issues you think they raise.

What can we learn from these children's ideas of reading?

Why not use the questionnaire in your classroom?

2 hours

TO BOLDLY GO...

Work on your own initially.

Study the snapshots of school life which are given in the extract below. As you read, note down some thoughts on the aspects of teaching and learning which represent quality and those which do not. Imagine you were walking into the classrooms. How do you think you would react?

When you have finished, share your responses with a colleague and then, as a pair, share again with another pair.

The nursery is prepared and ready for the children to arrive. As they enter there is a warm welcome from the adult who is on hand to greet them and they are invited to choose something that they would like to do. There is a range of options. Some children move immediately to the large climbing frame, others to the home corner which at present is set up as a hairdresser's salon; others begin to enjoy the table toys, while some children come in through one door and out through another to play on the large toys in the play area. Some children are somewhat hesitant and remain near to their parents. Parents are welcome and encouraged to stay for as long as the children need them or for as long as they feel they need to stay. The staff make a point of chatting easily with parents so that they feel that time is not limited or rationed and that there is always a listening ear if they have a pressing problem.

The nursery seems a happy place. Parents read picture books to their own and other children, and children seem to turn naturally to any available adult. A small group of boys begins to hammer nails into a slab of wood at the workbench. The water tray contains a brightly coloured liquid and the nursery nurse is encouraging a small group of children to talk about the changing effects as different coloured tissue paper is added.

A parent is busy with a group of children looking at differences in a bowl of fruit salad. Children talk of shape, colour, size and texture and they take examples from the bowl with tweezers. The parent makes a chart of their investigation and adds the title 'dehydration'. (They leave the fruit to see what will happen to it over the next few days.)

Just outside there is a group of blindfolded children gathered around the sand tray which is full of mud. Children are searching for objects which have been secreted in the mud and try to work out what they have found. Shrieks of delight and laughter fill the air.

Back inside, the hairdresser is busy and some children wait patiently, reading magazines. Others are content to make an appointment and return later.

The teacher makes some cups of tea for the adults and sits herself down in the rocking chair to cuddle Kate who just doesn't seem too happy today.

Now think about your discussion in pairs or small groups.

How far did your reactions compare?

What were the areas of agreement?

What were the areas of disagreement?

Were there aspects of the snapshots which you had read in a very different way from your colleagues?

Were there parts of the snapshots which had assumed more or less significance for you than for others?

It is very possible that you had entirely different perceptions and opinions about the snapshots. This is because each of us brings our own background and history to our teaching. We are selective in what we notice or place importance upon. When we discuss educational issues, we have to accept that everyone does not see the same picture from the same angle. We may be affected by our previous experience as a teacher or a pupil, by our training, interests and enthusiasms, by previous experiences with parents, by the resources we have had available, by the pressures we feel.

All these aspects of our teaching history lead us to develop our own philosophy, and this often persuades us to act in certain ways. Strongly held beliefs will be defended; less strongly held beliefs will be compromised under pressure from other sources. It is important that we try to understand each other's values and beliefs. Creating the opportunity for discussion is a way towards such understanding.

Here are two additional snapshots of school life.

In the main building the reception children have settled back down to work after their PE. The children are engaged in a variety of activities, spread across a large open area. Some groups are using construction materials, both junk and commercially produced. Four children are working with a parent on finger painting and at the water tray a small group of children is having a lovely time with some bubbly red water. A small group is looking closely with a teacher at the way a bicycle pump works and they are trying to do diagrams to show other children. The home corner has been converted into a garage and children in hard hats are jacking up cars and crawling underneath to pronounce the diagnosis. A girl walks past with a spanner and tells a boy to hurry up with the oil.

He wanders off and does a jigsaw puzzle. On the computer a girl is busy printing off copies of the story she has been writing and in the art area two children are talking themselves through some painting of the garage that their group visited recently. One teacher is listening to readers. Children come in turn to read and after a few pages the teacher marks their place on a card which is placed in the book. The teacher is very positive about reading and praises the children at great length as they finish a book, making a great fuss about the next book she is giving to the child.

The whole room vibrates with colour and lively displays. There are objects from olden days to look at, animals to care for, instruments to play, puzzles to do, experiments to try, games to play and the children seem to simply get on with it. There is a book on a teacher's table which holds the pattern of groups for the morning and, now and again, individual children come to see what lies in store for them. The two teachers quietly organise groups, the nursery nurse and three parents.

__The children__ return to the classroom after the mid-morning break and the middle junior class continues the science experiment that they began at 9 o'clock this morning.

They had been set the task of building a model boat that would travel a distance of three metres across the paddling pool which had been constructed in the middle of the classroom. Immediately following the explanation of the task the children had rushed into action, using a range of wood, yoghurt cartons, polystyrene tiles and cardboard, and had hacked away with the woodwork equipment, knives and other assorted instruments available. After a very short while Darren had approached the teacher and asked whether she had a pin he could use. The teacher, Jenny Carter, provided the pin and watched as Darren inflated three balloons and fixed them to the stern of his balsa boat. Having placed the boat on the water, Darren then proceeded to burst the balloons. The exasperation on his face when the boat remained stationary while everyone looked round on hearing the loud bang led to a long period of silence and then a repeat performance as he sensed that it was something to do with the quality of the balloons. Other children tried other tactics, but as yet nobody had managed to persuade their boat to move.

It had been difficult to encourage the children to go out to play and when they returned they had ceased to be active, but clustered in groups around the room discussing possibilities and trying out ideas and theories together. There is a good deal of perseverance and a good deal of frustration. Jenny Carter sits quietly watching.

Try to use another of these 'To boldly go...' snapshots as vehicles for exploring each other's perceptions of teaching and learning. Another possibility is for you 'to boldly go' into each other's classrooms and around the school. If you go boldly where no person has been before, and simply state what you see without qualitative comment or analysis, there will be a basis for discussion, both about the reason for noticing what was recorded and about the significance of the events in the snapshots.

Before we say where we are going, we need to work out where we start.

We have now reached a very important stage.

We have considered the climate in which we operate, the views of teachers, and the ways in which children view reading.

Now comes the moment when we have to stop, think and ask ourselves whether we are happy doing things as we are, or whether in fact we need to move our thinking and our approach on a little.

Sometimes teachers change their approach almost without realising it by gradually adjusting to new demands, to their own instinctive feelings, to children's enthusiasms. Then they suddenly realise they are teaching very differently.

ARE YOU SATISFIED WITH THE WAY IN WHICH YOUR SCHOOL TRIES TO HELP CHILDREN LEARN TO READ?

Taking stock can be refreshing. Stopping to consider and plan can ensure that new approaches have a significant chance of working effectively, because everyone involved is clear about the thinking behind the action.

This TIME OUT needs a good deal of time, which is why we suggest it as an INSET day. There are four stages to work through. Each stage needs considerable attention, and we hope you will go into it with the reading debate discussed in chapter one in your minds. Talking through the stages, the debate and the implications is good preparation for deciding how we might move forward. Too often we rush into action without really being aware of possible repercussions.

It is useful to work in groups of three. When you have discussed the questions posed at each stage, it is sensible for groups to compare their responses. The questions thus become a starting point for debate about the important stages of curriculum review in the approach to helping children learn to read.

At the end of the process, you will have shared with colleagues all sorts of ideas and concerns about how you should proceed. You will have revealed to colleagues some of your impressions of the way in which your school works or should work. You may have been surprised by what some people have said, and you may even have been surprised by some of the things you said. Well used, this activity will allow you to explore your own thoughts, and the whole staff to decide upon the most appropriate approach for the whole school.

Stage one: Planning   1   What do you intend should be the outcome of your efforts in teaching children to read by the time they are 11 years old?

2   In what ways can you ensure coherence and progression in the learning process?

3   In what ways should your approach to the teaching of reading be modified to take account of different children's

needs? (Children in multi-cultural schools, children with poor motor co-ordination, and so on.)

4 List three recent developments in thinking about children's early language development and the teaching of reading.

5 How can effective recording of children's reading progress best be achieved?

6 What aspects of children's reading development and progress should be recorded?

7 How do we identify children who have problems learning to read?

8 How are such children best helped?

9 In what ways can parents be involved and integrated into the school's approach to learning to read?

Stage two: The initiating process 1 Who should initiate a curriculum review? Suggest some people who may provoke a review.

2 What ways are available to find out what is happening about learning to read in your school?

3 How do we evaluate what is happening?

4 Who should take a lead?

5 Who decides whether new initiatives are necessary?

Stage three: Action 1 What methods are available for communicating the revised pattern of work?

2 What resources are necessary?

3 Who should obtain resources?

4 Who should help staff become familiar with new resources?

5 Who should oversee implementation?

6 How do we ensure pace and progress in implementation?

Stage four: 1 Looking back at its purpose, when should an evaluation
Evaluation be planned?

2 Who should evaluate?

3 Should evaluation be continuous? If not, what alternatives do you suggest?

4 How would evaluation be best achieved?

5 How do we measure improvement?

6 Who should reflect on improvement? What messages will show positive or negative implementation?

Chapter 4

MANAGING CHANGE
The challenge for
the school

Bringing about change is very difficult. Perhaps we should think carefully about whether this chapter title is accurate, and whether we are searching for change in education. Perhaps we are looking for something far more subtle: development rather than change.

The world of commerce might offer us a few pointers to the way in which we could promote new approaches in education. When seeking to sell a different brand of toothpaste or soap powder, companies rarely apologise for the old product or suggest that it was ineffective. Rather they talk of 'new formula' toothpaste or 'new improved' soap powder, and indicate that there is a ceaseless quest for improvement.

The Guardian newspaper ran a series of advertisements to prepare readers for its new format. Great efforts were made to stress the strengths of the newspaper, and to emphasise the way in which the new appearance and approach would enhance the product. Following the launch of the new look, the newspaper published many letters offering a range of readers' views, some positive and some negative. These emphasised the importance of the customer, and kept the new development in the news for as long as possible.

In education, we need to reach parents with the message that we are a profession constantly searching for developments which will offer children an enhanced opportunity to benefit fully from their school experience. We need to be wary of suggesting that a new approach represents the final answer, or that previous techniques were at fault. It must be made clear that our constant aim is to extend our thinking and our practice. We are looking for development.

Curriculum development does not just happen in schools.

It's three years since the idea was first mooted around The Guardian that might be possible to produce a newspaper like The Guardian, only better.

A newspaper with Guardian values; Guardian wit, personality and Guardian quality, but with more advanced styling, more effective organisation of editorial and innovative use of the technology becoming available.

Editors and journalists, specialist newspaper designers, printing technologists and software compilers discreetly set to work on this 'better' Guardian.

On Friday, February 12 we'll reveal to you the fruits of their labours.

The *new* Guardian.

With The Guardian's heart and The Guardian's mind; but brighter, fresher, easier to use and more enjoyable for you to read.

No one else has managed to produce a paper that's better than The Guardian, so we've decided to do it ourselves.

The new Guardian.
In our unbiased opinion, you'll love it.

If only it were that simple. It takes great effort and skill for a school to implement successfully a new policy or institute a change of approach. A number of challenges lie on the route to success and must be confronted and overcome in order to achieve development.

CHALLENGE NUMBER ONE: OWNERSHIP

Every so often in education, as in other fields, a buzz word comes along, a word that everyone seems to be using. 'Ownership' is such a word, and it deserves its vogue. The more teachers feel that they have a stake in a new development, the more successful it is likely to be.

The more that a teacher can claim to be responsible for an approach, the more energy, enthusiasm and commitment will follow. The challenge is to give people the responsibility and influence that will allow them to take the decisions which will help ensure that they can achieve their goals.

A class teacher with responsibility for language development told us:

The new approach changed the whole attitude to reading within the school. Children were dashing up to me wanting to read books, telling me about the books they'd read. From the reception class it went on into the other class and as the year progressed we introduced it into the middle-year class. Now, initially, the teacher in the middle year wasn't too happy but, when she saw the attitude of the children, then she was really enthusiastic and so it's really grown since then.

CHALLENGE NUMBER TWO: EROSION OF STATUS AND INFLUENCE

As the status of one person rises in a relationship, so the status of others often falls. This has serious implications for the school in the initiatives taken for development of curriculum ideals. If reading suddenly becomes a focus for development, then it is natural that the people responsible for other curriculum areas may feel that their influence is being eroded. While they may not be resistant, they will be aware that their interest is not central. If promotion is seen to depend upon making impact, then indeed there may be some resentment.

The new teacher to a school, especially if appointed to develop a specific area, can be seen as a threat to the status of others. A young teacher, fresh from college and enthusiastic about all the current thinking, can seem to be a challenge. But as the novice struggles to come to terms with the complexity of the job which is teaching, knowing looks and asides from colleagues can convince the novice that to become part of the group is more important than fighting for influence. It may not be long before the newcomer is heard to utter the same assumptions as the others — and the opportunity for development is lost in the search for acceptance.

Carol Green's work provides an example:

A member of staff most affected by the change was my infant helper, Mrs W, and at the time of the change I had no appreciation of what an asset she would prove to be. Her support has been total throughout the year but her profound knowledge of young children and her perceptive observations helped me enormously, especially in discerning emerging reading behaviour. She has also had excellent ideas on how to change the circular record to better suit our purposes. She had very little experience of working with reading schemes and was very open-minded.

Mrs H, the other infant teacher, has firmly held views on reading which seem to run contrary to Frank Smith's. Several issues worried her about the new approach. Lack of accuracy in reading particularly bothered her and the extent to which reading from real books depends on memory and already knowing the story. These are very real issues for her to come to terms with before she can appreciate the gains. This approach has a different value system. The changes in behaviour of the reader are the gains, the children's attitudes are so very important. The number of books does not matter — although it will probably be higher. Mrs H, although sceptical about this method, has made considerable moves towards reading from real books. She has included library books in her reading stock and is allowing her children more freedom of choice in what they read.

CHALLENGE NUMBER THREE: DESKILLING

Sometimes, when we move our thinking forward and develop different ways of working, we need to use different skills. This often means that in the quest for progress we do not call upon some of the skills we have been using before. Relinquishing them is not always a simple and painless process.

Many an excellent cook has been caught crying into the

new microwave, unable to understand why years of experience should now appear invalid as a tried and tested recipe fails. Many a labour-saving gadget is stored away in a cupboard while the owner continues to use the old-fashioned techniques. Indeed, many of us are reluctant to try to come to terms with technology.

Drivers will know the feeling associated with deskilling if they imagine sitting in an unfamiliar car with the engine running while they try to find the reverse gear. Passers-by look quizzical as the engine revs up, the car edges slightly forward and then stops. The driver, aware of the spectacle being created, frantically searches for the correct gear position, but concedes defeat when the car nearly nudges a car in front. Covered with embarrassment, the driver experiences further humiliation by the need to consult someone else. The ultimate blow comes when the other driver says how easy it is, but is quite unable to explain the technique because it is so routine and automatic.

A good example of issues related to deskilling occurred in education on the introduction of open-plan schools. Around the time of 'Plowden' some teachers, mainly in smaller schools, decided that they could offer a more appropriate curriculum by working together in a more flexible way. In some cases they found it easier to remove doors and partitions to create the conditions which were favourable to the way they wanted to work. They were committed to working in this way, having ownership, and they achieved a considerable degree of success. When observers tried to unravel the secret, the opportunities created by the variable use of space were seen to be important.

Many new schools were then designed as open plan, and teachers confronted a new set of challenges. After a successful teaching career in traditional classrooms, a whole set of skills were inappropriate and a whole set of new skills were needed. Some teachers so deskilled found themselves unable to work effectively under the scrutiny of colleagues. Unfortunately, expertise was not widespread. Few advisers had any experience of open-plan schools, and the only real avenue for learning was to observe schools which seemed to be operating effectively with the open plan. For the deskilled visitor to spend time at the smoothly operating open-plan school was often demoralising, serving to emphasise inadequacy. This feeling was heightened as the teachers who were working happily in the open-plan school struggled to explain techniques, finally suggesting that their teaching was natural. In fact, they had tuned routines so successfully that they were unable to articulate the starting points for their thinking, the very starting points needed by the novices.

Little wonder that the deskilled teachers began to revert to techniques which had served them well in the past. Book racks, coat trolleys and assorted furniture were carefully positioned to recreate enclosed classrooms within the open plan. Opinions were voiced that open plan does not work for everyone, and that the teacher who succeeds needs a special quality associated with a quaint form of purgatory. Of course, the poor teacher who has retrenched in the 'class base' is bound to feel frustrated by the distraction of the rest of the school, by working in a space less well designed than a traditional classroom, and by a niggling sense of failure to adapt to the open-plan approach.

If we translate the deskilling concept into the context of reading, there are lessons to be learned. However much a teacher can appreciate the value of adopting a different approach to helping children to learn to read, a considerable challenge awaits anyone who has the nerve to try. For example, to remove reading schemes is to remove all many teachers have known as a pupil and teacher. As the reading schemes are taken away, so are security and confidence, and without these the teacher may be hard-pressed to encourage children to take the learning risk. Few teachers rely totally on reading schemes. Possibly without even realising, teachers will have developed a battery of skills and techniques to support their work alongside whatever materials they are using. Nonetheless, if they see the schemes as being their approach, they will feel vulnerable upon discontinuing the schemes. Glib assertions that using 'real' books is an obvious and natural approach will not offer this teacher the sort of climate to encourage taking the learning risk that the development involves. While the teacher may not reject the new approach entirely, it is very likely that a compromise will be sought in which the teacher can at least feel capable. The challenge is to sustain the teacher while the new approach is tried, and to reassure and support if feelings of inadequacy occur.

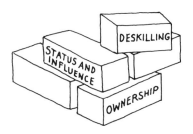

CHALLENGE NUMBER FOUR: ONLY ONE TEACHER ON THE COURSE

The challenge of the course attender returning to school is significant. Anyone who has worked for a head teacher who regularly attends weekend short courses will appreciate the impact of the aftermath. If the course is calligraphy, pens and ink will be needed. If it is science, magnifying glasses and microscopes should be on standby; if it is music, tambourines are at the ready; if it is dance, leotards are the order of the day.

Apart from being a source of ideas and suggestions, a

course can create a serious challenge as a member of staff returns to school fired with enthusiasm. The returning teacher exclaims about the week away while the rest of the staff remembers the battles to cover the absence, cope with wet playtimes and struggle through the crises that always seem to arise. Little wonder that there may be scant interest in the discoveries from the course, especially if one of them is how everyone else has been going wrong. As Carol Green recalled:

When I arrived back at school after the course at Lincoln, I was fired with enthusiasm and eager to tell everyone about it. They were in the last week of a long spring term and tired out...spreading the influence of such a good course isn't easy. We have reporting-back sessions in staff meetings but that isn't very satisfactory. We need to share in-service training as a staff to feel the real impact of a course.

The challenge facing the school in terms of using people who attend courses is an important one. Coupled with this challenge is how to cope with the 'born-again' teacher. In terms of reading, the teacher who has seen the light can drive people to despair. Every time a member of staff so much as mentions the topic of reading the record begins, accompanied by a zealous imploring of everyone to join in the search for the new world. The most tolerant of people can reject the ideas being given because of the way in which they are offered.

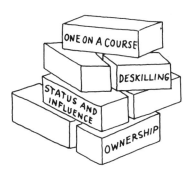

CHALLENGE NUMBER FIVE: ONE TEACHER SEEN AS THE EXPERT

The expert can actually delay development, however unwittingly. Sometimes the expert is self-appointed, sometimes acknowledged, sometimes respected, sometimes tolerated, sometimes ignored. Whatever the situation, the expert has to have a high level of skill in dealing with people in order to ensure that development takes place. It is so easy for people to leave the work to the expert. If they have no ownership of the new approach, they will tolerate it as long as no-one puts too much pressure upon them.

A common example in primary schools is that of the nomadic music teacher, peddling the piano from class to class with nobody else either involved or interested. The same phenomena began to develop in the early days of micros in schools, but it seems that the knowledge and expectations of children meant that the myth of proficiency being the preserve of one or two adults was dispelled.

The problem with the expert operating apart from others is that ownership of the approach is too exclusive. The others fail to realise that ownership is available and prefer to allow the expert to continue to dispense the expertise.

The increasing number of advisory teachers who have worked in schools have had as a remit the job of encouraging others to take on the skills. There is an understanding that their aim is to generate activity and involvement rather than to do the work for the school.

The challenge facing the school is not how to use the expert, but how to use the expertise of the expert.

CHALLENGE NUMBER SIX: THE DANGER
OF THE CHECKLIST

Given some of the challenges of trying to develop new approaches, it is natural that less certain teachers will seek to ensure that they are covering the demands made. A safe way to match efforts to demands is the checklist itemising the stages of development. It is normal for teachers to believe that they should have a checklist of skills or concepts in order to record the progress that the children are making. The danger here is that the checklist ceases to be a record and instead becomes a planned programme through which all children are expected to proceed. The record sheet becomes a straightjacket for teacher and child alike. Beyond this, in spite of all the time teachers spend on them, the checklists can become impossible to maintain with the hundreds of items to be entered on a regular basis. Realistically, teachers can do little more than complete such lists on a football pools basis, hoping that occasionally they will permutate the right combination.

Even without the burden of the formal checklist, the teacher may often resort to a hierarchical order. Within the area of early reading, teachers who have moved away from the structure of reading schemes may seek to order the reading experience of children by systematising the materials used. Colour coding of books, shelving arrangements, and grouping of children are all methods of ordering the learning experience. Before too long they can all become methods for constraining the experience and limiting the flexibility which was sought. The struggle for simplicity can outface both the teacher and the learner in emphasising the size of the task that lies ahead.

Children are quick to sense that they are on a series of steps when they embark upon learning to read, whether there is a formal ordering or a subtle, intuitive one.

One of our students was researching her extended study in an infant classroom using a 'real book' approach, having abandoned traditional schemes. She left a tape recorder running in the reading corner. Children were heard to say things like:

"When you finish that one you can have What a mess.*"*

"I know why she likes reading... 'cause you only have to read so many and then you can go on to the next lot."

What it seems was happening was that the teachers, trying to move forward with developments had, almost subconsciously, ordered the books. The children had somehow picked this up from the way the teachers responded to them and were forming ideas about the choices available.

The challenge facing the school is that of resisting the urge to formalise and simplify a process which is complex, unpredictable and uncertain in the eyes of so many.

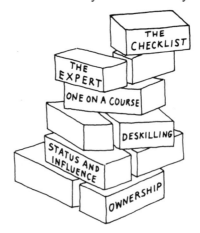

CHALLENGE NUMBER SEVEN: FINDING RESOURCES

Serious consideration needs to be given at the planning stage to the reading resources needs of the school. Too often schools plan in the short term, flooding the place with new materials. Reading schemes are attractive because they are relatively cheap for the number of books offered and, supplemented by a carefully selected range of other materials, represent realistic spending. But without long-term planning, worn stock cannot be replaced and the initiative is doomed to failure. Morale drops as materials deteriorate and cannot be updated. The progress of the children is slowed down or thwarted. Staff are not convinced of the commitment to the development. Then the school is faced with a dilemma. Should it move on to yet another initiative which might not be adequately resourced? Or should it replace the reading scheme, a costly project which might deflect finance from other valuable resources?

Resource provision extends beyond money and materials to human resources, which are the most valuable commodity available to the school. The expertise and professional commitment of teachers is the key to success. The challenge facing the school is to harness the available skills and talents and to build a team able to make maximum use of material resources. The planning of in-service work becomes important, both as to the training of teachers to research new approaches and the opportunity within school to share skills with other staff.

Other staff need support from all concerned to offer the best chance of success. The concern for status and the issue of ownership often mean that schools tend to share around resources rather than institute long-term plans.

CHALLENGE NUMBER EIGHT: KEEPING A SENSE OF PROPORTION

There is a danger that, as a school begins a wholehearted effort to develop one aspect of its work, it does so at the neglect of others. We all know schools that have built a reputation, deservedly or not, for excellence in a certain area of the curriculum: the 'art' or 'science' schools, or the schools that year after year produce the best football team in the area, or the best choir at the music festival. Learning to read, strangely, carries less prestige. Few schools are known for the excellence of their work with children who find reading difficult. We may want to become the school known for reading achievement. In doing so, however, there is a danger that other important aspects of work get dismissed or forgotten. We get carried away with our successes rather than puzzling over the odd child who has not found the new initiative provides the answer. We enthuse with those who are with us and forget to talk to those who do not understand. We can become dismissive and resentful that everyone cannot see the wonders that we see being performed.

Every new voyage needs a good launch but sometimes those at sea need rescue. We must maintain a sense of proportion. Given enough enthusiasm and encouragement, children will seek to show teachers how much they are achieving within the confines arranged by the teacher: the prophecy will be self-fulfilling, played back to the teacher by the children who know it is needed. But we must not, in our exuberance or our genuine belief, delude ourselves into thinking that there is only one way forward. It is a mistake that has been made too often. A philosophy should be strong and firmly defended. An approach or method should enable the philosophy and not dictate to it. The extremist views on the teaching of reading are often not concerned with philosophy or belief, but with defending previous practice and refusing to recognise that thinking moves on.

The challenge facing the school is to keep a sense of proportion and to take a calculated, dispassionate look at progress at regular intervals.

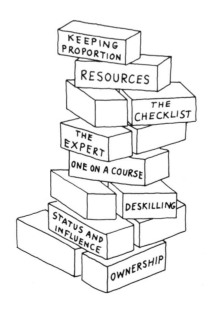

CHALLENGE NUMBER NINE: KEEPING IT GOING

With all the other challenges bearing down upon the school, it requires great resilience, forethought and planning to ensure that the new developments can be maintained. In many ways the only way to ensure further development is to meet the other challenges successfully. To create a sense of ownership, to avoid status difficulties, to overcome deskilling issues, to spread the expertise, to provide appropriate resources and to keep a sense of proportion is the daunting challenge to further progress. If schools make a move forward in the curriculum and then come to a standstill, there is usually a reason. The reason is most likely to be associated with the challenges.

The prime mover becomes fed up: nobody wants to share the ownership; the expert leaves; the emphasis gets out of hand; the school is overwhelmed and needs a break; resources dry up. All these are problems to be anticipated and avoided.

The challenge of maintaining further development is most easily met by trying to ensure that, from the start, the development is a corporate act by as many people as possible. Where there is an individual initiative, action may occur but it is likely to be temporary. Where there is a collective approach, a policy is more likely to emerge and the prospects for continuing development are considerably enhanced.

CHALLENGE NUMBER TEN: PARENTAL PERCEPTION

Parents often display their just concern for their children at school. The more a school can engage the parent in the learning of the child, the greater the possibility of a successful collaboration for the child's benefit.

The challenge facing the school is trying to demonstrate to parents that the developments due to take place are a natural extension of the work being done already, and not a sudden whim or fancy. They need to know how educational thought has changed and why the methods that succeeded for them are not considered appropriate for their children. They need to know about this before new initiatives happen.

Schools so often make changes which seem sensible to them but which baffle parents. The assumption that parents will understand and accept new approaches is a dangerous one. Parents might accept them as long as children seem to be making progress, even without understanding, but they will certainly not accept them if children seem to be faltering. Parents who are worried, even about different things, can unite to attack a change at the school as a tangible target.

Immediately the school can be on the defensive, fighting a rearguard action to convince the unwilling of the value of a particular approach and always answering random questions rather than presenting a reasoned case.

One of the head teachers in our survey, (see chapter three), told us of her experience in trying to develop an approach which placed less reliance upon traditional reading schemes:

We had been operating 'real book' techniques for some time and we were very pleased with the way things were going generally. Then, for some reason or other a rumour started to go around that we weren't teaching reading any more and that the children could choose whether they read to the teacher or not. Agitation started to grow and some parents began to ask questions of one of the teachers. She felt vulnerable, caught on the hop, and acted defensively which only served to cause more problems, with the more articulate parents really stirring it up. They accused us of using their children as guinea pigs. We eventually had a parents' evening and a visiting speaker talked about learning to read. We were able to talk to them and reassure them of our concern. If we were to make other changes I have realised that it is important to take the parents with you. The best thing we have done is to buy some copies of books about reading to loan to parents. Once they read these they realise that what we are doing makes sense. I'd really recommend a library of educational books for parents.

The way forward seems obvious: to involve parents fully, from the beginning, and to give to them the belief in the new approach which will transmit confident learning to their children. But we all know that the obvious is not always easy. There will always be the awkward parents who maintain that what was good enough for them is good enough for their children — and who are we to suggest that they did not learn properly at school? Neither do schools have access to marketing technology. If only we could advertise our 'new-formula' approach to reading!

We can, though, as is suggested at the beginning of this chapter, work to assure parents that we are constantly seeking to develop our understanding of learning and teaching, and that any new technique used is carefully evaluated.

It is possible to convince an open mind with a carefully presented case; but it takes much more to convince doubters who have already decided that the case is full of holes.

With all these daunting and overlapping challenges facing the school, it is a wonder that we ever make progress or introduce new approaches. In preparing for new developments, the school must anticipate and prepare to confront challenges. One or more of the ten listed here are bound to arise. Forewarned is forearmed...

TIME OUT

30 minutes

Look carefully at these typical statements. Try to match the statements with the 10 challenges discussed in the chapter. Indicate if you think the statement represents more than one challenge. (This is often the case.) First work on your own and then compare your analysis with that of a colleague.

1 It's all right for you. You're just starting out. Spare a thought for us old-fashioned workers.

2 It's all very well, but parents need to know that their child is making progress.

3 I've put all the books on a card system and at least I'm able to keep track of who is on what book and what they need to read next.

4 I've seen new ideas before. I prefer to stay off the bandwagon and wait for the pendulum to swing back.

5 Try as I might, I still cannot believe that this new approach is any better than the way we have been working for years.

6 I know it works, it works for me. Why can't you see the obvious advantages?

7 It's fine for people like you. You've worked in schools where this approach is quite normal. For people like us it is not so simple.

8 I just do as I'm told. It saves having to get involved in all the hassle.

9 I've never felt as unsure as I do now.

10 The children are so keen to borrow the books to take

home that I don't have enough for use in class. I start a rota system.

11   I'm absolutely sick of all this talk about reading. I was a problem, it isn't a problem now and I just d .ot understand all the fuss.

12   It was good before Judy left. We were all enthusiastic but now there seem to be other priorities.

13   If I get asked whether he is progressing well one more time, I'll go mad. Can't she see he is reading and enjoying books?

14   You hardly dare ask. Joyce seems so capable and finds everything so easy, she'll think I'm terrible if I say I can't cope.

15   Who does she think she is? Straight from college and trying to tell us how to teach. She'll learn!

GET READY

Try to think of a change of practice in your classroom which did not continue or develop in the way it was anticipated. Note it down.

Next, note down the reasons why the new approach floundered. Try to tease out as many as you can. Some reasons will obviously relate to others, some will stand alone.

Using your list of reasons, chat with colleagues about the developments which were dropped.

Try to match your reasons for failure with the 10 challenges outlined in chapter four.

By talking about the challenges in the light of your list of reasons for the discontinuance of a change, you will become more aware of the complexity of the issues surrounding any policy change. To sustain a change is difficult. We must address the issues rather than hope they do not occur. Previous experience assists us to do so.

Chapter 5

FACING
THE CHALLENGES

Once we identify some of the challenges likely to face us in managing a new reading development, it is sensible to think of ways in which we might address those challenges in order to implement the proposed new approach.

Action number one: Know where you are and where you want to be Too often we set off without knowing what we want to achieve. Perhaps we did not know we were setting

off at all because a new pattern of work emerged naturally from a previous approach. It is important to take stock and think about our goals. If we know where the journey is leading us, then we are likely to think about where we are starting from. We are likely to anticipate some of the challenges that lie on the way. We can begin by recognising exactly how big or how small the development is.

TIME OUT

1 hour

PIE IN THE SKY

Draw yourself a diagram on a sheet of A4 paper of pie in the sky, like the one opposite. The bottom crust should be a box. Think carefully about the way in which your school tries to help children learn to read.

If you could wave a magic wand and make some aspect of your work perfect, what would it be? What, above everything else, would you wish your school could get sorted out?

When you have decided, write it down as a simple phrase in the pie crust box. You might, for example, put 'full parental involvement'.

Next, think about the relationship between this ideal and the practice in your school. Describe it in a short statement and write it in a box at the bottom of the page. You might, for example, put 'no parents show interest'.

With a colleague, you now need to question the statement you have written in the bottom box. The questions need to explore the exact position of the bottom box:

How do I know?
What is my evidence?
Who says this is the position? Just me, or several others?

The point of these questions is to try to establish exactly where you stand before you try to move towards the desired goal. You need to know precisely whether you are taking on a major task or a small adjustment. You should assume nothing, but subject yourself to a rigorous examination to try to reveal the distance that has to be covered.

Full parental involvement

No parents show interest

Caroline Ewen

As you define the starting point, you will become aware of the extent of the gap between the bottom and top boxes. The size of this gap is the size of the task.

The gap between current and better practice is what we can call the 'performance gap'.

The aim of any action we take in trying to develop practice is to reduce the performance gap. The smaller we can make the gap, the nearer we are to fulfilling our educational beliefs.

Of course, we need to recognise that, as we close the gap, our goal may move upwards. The aim is to try to bring the two boxes as close together as possible. Perhaps we have to recognise that there should always be a slight performance gap. We constantly raise our sights, and so we should if a feeling of complacency is not to develop because there is nothing left for which to strive.

Initially, the top box can seem an extremely long way off — pie in the sky. We need to recognise this from the beginning. We need to realise that the performance gap is a big one and that an enormous amount of work lies ahead. It is better to know the extent of the task from the beginning rather than to suddenly realise it and feel outfaced.

We need our dreams, our pie in the sky. But we also need a sense of realism to make our dreams possible.

Having found out where we are and where we want to be, it makes sense to look around and see what we can build on. So often schools attempt to develop areas for which they are not equipped, and neglect developments which would be perfectly possible by using and moving on from the areas in which they have achieved success. The skill is to identify precisely what it is that makes a particular aspect of the school's work positive and rewarding.

Action number two: Recognise the strengths that might help If we can identify precisely what it is that makes an aspect of the school good, then we can use that strength to develop other aspects.

Maybe it is the way resources are provided; or the enthusiasm and knowledge of particular teachers; or the involvement of parents; or the space available; or the co-operation of the whole staff. Whatever it is, this is the strength upon which we can build.

SOMETHING GOOD

Draw a box about the size of a matchbox in the centre of an A4 sheet of paper.

Think very carefully about an aspect of the work of your

school which represents quality, something that you feel the school should be pleased to recognise. Write it down in a couple of words within the box.

Find a colleague to question you about this aspect of school. The questioning needs to be ruthless and rigorous so that you cannot get away with easy answers. For example:

Why do you say this is good?
How do you know?
What is the evidence?
How do you know it is an improvement?
What do you mean by well organised?

While these questions are being answered, the colleague can note key points around the original box.

At the end of this process, study the paper carefully. What will have emerged are some of the aspects of your school which underpin the quality you already have.

If we can look closely at our school and identify what it is that is really good, and then look for the foundation upon which that is built, we are able to establish our strengths. It is by building on our strengths that we have the greatest chance of success.

Another important issue is that we can be haphazard about identifying exactly what factors make an initiative work within a school. So often, visiting teachers to a school can sense that there is something good happening, that real quality is apparent. However, they clutch at what it might be that causes the quality, sometimes with wreckless imprecision. They look for what is different from their own circumstances: the furniture, the display paper, the time of day, and take the recognisable difference back to their own situation without teasing out the implications. They adopt a sort of 'Burglar Bill' approach: "That's a nice bookshelf, I'll have that!" or "That's a nice coloured display board. I'll have that!" or "That's a nice way of using parents, I'll have that!" What this does is to isolate one feature without really appreciating the combination of features important to the quality. By too much simplifying, we can overlook the foundation upon which the strength depends. We are in danger of missing the point.

Too often schools try to move forward without playing to the strength, and realise too late that the planned development cannot succeed because the necessary skills are not available.

If we use the strengths we identify, then we are working upon people's confidence. This is a far more positive way forward than trying to overcome failings.

Having looked carefully at actions number one and two, and considered the range of issues associated with what we want to develop, there is a need to plan a strategy with calculated precision and to anticipate the challenges that lie ahead. Things may still go awry, but at least a plan will help to get us back on course after any hiccups.

As teachers, we are often said to be 'nurturing the young', so we might find an analogy useful. Gardeners often proudly show their plants and announce: "Look what I've grown." Of course, this is only partly true. The plants grew themselves, but the gardener's role is crucial. The gardener nurtures the growth of the plants so that they reach full maturity and beauty. Both gardening and teaching require constant attention and adjustment to varying conditions which are not always favourable.

Action number three: Prepare the ground and sow the seeds
If the bloom is to be worth cutting, then the seeds have to have the best possible start. If we want to develop our approach to reading, there has to be a lot of spade work before we begin. As gardeners do, we need to get many factors right before we expose the seed to the elements. We need to review the range of materials available, the space to be used, the time issues, the parents' and the children's perceptions. So often we fail to talk with the children concerned about why we are asking them to engage in an

activity. They have to try to deduce what is important in the work they do. They make all sorts of deductions, usually based upon the teacher's response at the end of the activity. Enlightening them in advance is a bit like using good fertiliser.

This might be a useful stage to decide what we are going to do without if we are to take on a new initiative. Just as the gardener needs land to lie fallow every now and then, we need to ensure that we do not overload the curriculum, the teachers, the parents, or the children with new initiatives. An Aladdin approach to school development, borrowed from the popular panto, could be useful: 'new lamps for old'. If we are going to trade in an old lamp for a new one, which one is most expendable? We cannot continually take on every new idea that forces itself on education; we have to be realistic.

The final, and perhaps most important, aspect of preparing the ground is to ensure that everyone is clear about the definition of success. The seed packet must contain a picture of the crop. We need to know what success will look like. Nor is it any use just measuring how we will recognise success and what the possible side shoots could be. We need to know what to prune back and where there will be a need for a support.

A considerable investment needs to be made in terms of promoting the development within and outside school. A confident start can be made if there is an air of expectation.

This does not mean that the start has to be accompanied by fanfares and trumpets. A quiet start is often best, but it needs to be planned.

Confidence can grow if efforts are made to provide the skills before the work begins, if teachers get the chance to talk with people who have developed the new approach and get the opportunity to talk about the challenges and not just the obvious successes.

Confidence can grow if there is an air of anticipation about the development and the self concept of the school is high. The way of promoting the development is significant. Like gardening, the promotion needs much gentle tilling of the soil and riddling out of stones.

Action number four: Anticipate the problems The gardener is always on the lookout for any threat to immature and treasured buds, constantly reviewing and overseeing the conditions. We need to check whether the climate is right. If not, we need to protect the growth and not allow shoots to wither in the face of the challenges we know exist. The gardener might place a cloche over the seedlings, shielding them from the harsh conditions. Sometimes we need to shield ourselves from undue attack.

A useful example of the cloche principle within the field of language development, though not specifically reading, is outlined by Simon Adorion, a teacher involved with the National Writing Project:

My class were working on a project producing books for infants, working alongside the mothers of the younger children. It was a superb project with all sorts of spin-offs. Parents and children working collaboratively, real purpose, real audience. Some of my class were running a creche for the babes. Then a few of the parents of children in my class started to get a bit bothered about the basics. They could see the point of all the writing, even the creche, but what about the basics? I had a chat with the class and we agreed a compromise, a sort of conspiracy. Each day, as quickly as we could, we would get on with the basics like fractions. Then we could get down to the real work. The children thought it was great. What was amazing was that we could do so much in such a short time just to get it out of the way. Perhaps it's not all that educational but it kept everyone happy.

We need to anticipate such problems and be ready with the cloches to help the shoots through difficult periods.

Another problem with any new development is the possibility of the irritating pests, the 'educational greenfly' which can take many forms. Just as the gardener knows what sort of cure to use for pests, so the school has to be aware of how to prevent minor irritations destroying the crop.

Many a teacher has given up on a potentially superb piece of curriculum development after being confronted by one moaning parent, not thinking that many other parents were probably quietly satisfied and supportive. The aggressive parent can have a powerful and debilitating effect upon the inexperienced teacher and can reduce the effectiveness of any new initiative.

We need to prepare ourselves for such onslaughts. We need not become so thick-skinned as to ignore the points made, but we do need to recognise that in any new development there will be those who are not happy. If we are convinced that the philosophy is strong and the approach appropriate, this can be equivalent to the spray or powder with which to fight off the educational greenfly.

Action number five: Nurturing the growth Once a plant has taken root and is established, it is very easy to neglect it. The good gardener continues to give attention and notices both growth and relapse. We have to do the same when a

new initiative has taken root. We should be prepared to offer support, whether the need comes from sudden strong growth or from sudden vulnerability due to an unexpected storm. Here is a telling note from one teacher's personal journal:

This has been the sort of week when everything has gone wrong. It shakes your belief in what you are doing and makes you question every assumption you have made about reading in the past. When filling in the children's circular record, quite a substantial proportion of children appeared to make little or no progress. Their reading behaviours had not changed significantly. I really needed to talk to someone who had been through the same crisis, but that wasn't possible.

I don't think any other change in my teaching methods has ever required such an act of faith by me, or taken as much conviction on my part. There are many people to whom I could turn for support; most of them believe in this method but have not been through the process with a class of children. I really needed a 'users support group' this week with a 24-hour hot line. Perhaps I should set one up!

Teachers need recognition for their work and they need to feel that their efforts are being noticed. Reassurance, time and energy need to be constantly available, sometimes only to regraft a broken shoot but other times to repot the whole uprooted plant.

Action number six: Enjoying the harvest Why do teachers deny themselves the pleasure of enjoying their achievements? They work so hard and contribute so much personal and professional commitment to helping children to learn. Yet, so often, they reduce the value of their own efforts. It is right that they should acknowledge the achievements of the child but it is also right that they should appreciate their own.

Teaching by its nature is a problem-solving activity and, for the effective teacher, the solution to one problem opens up more. The teaching and learning problems never disappear.

This can lead to an outlook which constantly emphasises the challenges we face rather than the achievements we have made. It is possible for the good teacher of the good school to give an impression that success is limited, that there are endless faults with the teaching and that improvement is desperately needed. Teachers, like children, need to recognise what they have accomplished and to enjoy the sweet smell of success, the fragrance of the bloom. If we do not actually gather the harvest, we will not be aware that we have grown a successful crop.

Beyond this we need to demonstrate to a wider audience just what the new approach has achieved. We must celebrate and enjoy the achievements of our children. Occasionally, we have to stop looking at what remains to be done and focus instead upon what has been accomplished. We have to

support each other, throughout the school, as we try to extend the boundaries of our understanding.

Above all, we have to try to hold on to what people are doing right. Whether relating to children or adults, we must notice the good. So often, people do not understand what the important aspects of their work are. By catching people doing things right, we establish priorities in a positive manner. This is a message that transmits from the classroom to the Secretary of State: catch people doing things right.

If we want to make real development in reading approaches, even before we begin we have to anticipate success and prepare to enjoy the fruit of our efforts: to reap the harvest.

KNOW WHERE YOU ARE—WHERE DO YOU WANT TO BE?
IDENTIFY A STRENGTH
PREPARE THE GROUND AND SOW THE SEED
ANTICIPATE THE PROBLEMS
NURTURE THE GROWTH
ENJOY THE HARVEST

STAFF AUDIT

Before beginning the process of making new developments, it is useful to consider the strengths that lie within the teaching team. If you do this, you will probably find that the human resources are comprehensive, even though a few gaps may become evident. In any event, it is better to be aware of the team's strengths and concerns before the development begins.

A staff audit is a helpful exercise. It need not take long to complete and can lead to a careful consideration of the strong points and needs.

STAFF AUDIT SHEET: HELPING CHILDREN TO LEARN TO READ

teacher	background	belief	experience	qualities	qualifications	skills	uncertainties
Peter	multi-cultural experience	Frank Smith etc.		enjoys teaching reading	Reading Diploma O.U.		organisational
Linda	nursery experience	real readers	lots of schools	well read on reading; studied for B.Ed.	B.Ed.	good organiser good communicator	whole staff commitment?

PLEASE WRITE SOME COMMENTS IN THE BOXES

As a group, try to fill in a grid like the one which we have begun as an example. When you have finished, think if there are other people not on the staff who could be added to your audit — perhaps a parent, an adviser or a local college lecturer might be a resource.

WHAT CAN GO WRONG

At this point we need a TIME OUT to prepare ourselves for the challenges that lie ahead. We can have the very best ideas for development, born of the best motives; but as we bring them into action, there will be pitfalls, minefields of problems to negotiate.

If, as a staff, we have decided to take certain actions, we can now realise the extent of the development by thinking of all the things that could go wrong.

On a large sheet of paper, work together to build up a list of all the threats to the success of this development. Does this sound like a sure way to fill everybody with gloom and doom? In fact, it does not have to be gloomy. You can have a good laugh envisaging the disasters that lie ahead. Much better to see them in the mind than in reality!

When the list is completed, decide which threats are serious or could become serious without due attention, and then lay plans to overcome them.

This the fun part. By working together we can actually come up with plans, strategies, diversions, smoke screens, under-cover work, head-on assaults. We become operators rather than responders.

If this TIME OUT is approached positively, a meeting about all the things that can go wrong can be exciting, creative and enjoyable; and it can weld together a fighting force.

Chapter 6

PRACTICAL
SUGGESTIONS

Now we come to the point of asking, "If I am developing my ideas of reading, how can I make a start, how can I organise for a different approach to reading without neglecting all the other valuable activities in my classroom?"

In the first part of chapter three we wrote about children's early language learning at home and in the community. The importance of talking with children and of reading and telling stories cannot be overstressed. Schools often get in touch with parents before their children start school to make contact and to encourage them to read and talk with their child. So let's begin the practical suggestions in this chapter by thinking about getting in touch with parents.

When teachers meet with parents in school or at home, they may:

- explain to parents about the school's approach to reading;
- suggest how parents could read and talk about books with their children;
- offer parents book lists;
- operate a lending library sometimes with cassette tapes and books together;
- encourage parents to write with their children.

An explanation of the school's approach to reading can be reassuring as well as informative. Some parents may well be wondering if they should be teaching their pre-school child to read or write and, if so, how they should go about it. Some simply go ahead and do it. Both will appreciate an understanding of the school's thinking.

We are becoming more experienced in sharing our ideas with parents. Sometimes schools make videos of children in the reception class to give parents an idea of what goes on. This often focuses on reading and books. Often parents and children are invited into school to see for themselves. They might join in with a story-and-rhyme time and explore the book corner. Teachers can take the opportunity of talking with parents and give them any available literature about the school's reading approach or lend them some of the published materials about early reading and writing.

Sometimes the reception class teacher or the head talks about reading and writing when they visit children's homes prior to the child joining the school. Some schools run workshops on reading, writing and maths for parents, giving them some ideas to try with their children at home. All these activities take up a good deal of time and require adequate organisation, but schools who have done it feel that the effort is well repaid. Parents immediately feel valued as an agent in their child's education, and this can but be for the good of all.

Sometimes schools offer parents book lists. These are obviously not prescriptive, the best books being those that parents and children enjoy together. Lists are helpful, though, for buying books or for borrowing from the library. Maybe the school runs a bookshop or a toddlers' lending library. This is a real help for busy parents and also an incentive to keep them in touch with the school. Sometimes parents wonder if they should buy the reading scheme material available in shops to give their children a good start. We would probably advise them not to, and offer alternative suggestions. We need to get across the message that enjoying books together is the best way to set children up both for reading at school and as readers for life.

If your school approach is to move away from dependence on reading schemes, it is all the more important to explain the change and your thinking to the parents of incoming children. They will then know what to expect. Otherwise they are going to be very puzzled, especially if they have had older children at school who have experienced the controlled and structured materials of a scheme. Parents will be much more confident if you can present the argument and the explanation in a firm yet lively way.

A head teacher writes:

When discussing our approach to reading with parents of the reception class, their reactions have often depended on their own experiences either as readers themselves or as parents with older children. Many of the older children had learned from a combination of phonics and a rigid reading scheme. In their minds the security of a reading scheme is coupled with the knowledge of success using this method. Their older children had learned to read so why were changes necessary?

I have talked openly about my experiences of helping my own children to read before I was trained as a teacher: my mistakes, frustrations and regret that I did not know what I know now.

This has led to some interesting revelations from the parents of their experiences with these older children. Some admitted to boredom as the children hesitatingly picked their way through dry, uninteresting and repetitive books, or tension and anxiety especially when their children appeared to forget words that they had previously known or when they were on 'lower' books than other children in the same class. Some even mentioned becoming so exasperated that they had thrown the reading book across the room or become angry with the child. These outbursts were invariably followed by feelings of guilt and remorse.

Reading and writing go together at school and at home. There are many opportunities for parents and children to write together. They often occur quite naturally through everyday situations like writing letters and cards, shopping lists, telephone messages, reminders. Children like very much to learn to write their names.

Sometimes parents initiate the writing and invite the children to join in. Other times children show parents what they have 'written' and parents take up from there. If it is an event or a story, they might offer to write the next part for the child. Writing together in this way is a very valuable activity. The child's 'writing' will be a mixture of squiggles and pictures at first, developing gradually through practice and guidance. Children gain insights about writing, too — that it carries a message and is therefore a means of communication, and that it is permanent as opposed to talk.

Children also learn from the print which is almost everywhere in the environment — in supermarkets, in the High Street, on television. Schools try to make parents aware of the ways in which children can learn reading from their environment. We will be returning to the role of parents later in this chapter.

There are many different ways in which schools can communicate with parents before the child's formal education begins. Teachers can explain, demonstrate, show, read and lend books and encourage shared reading and writing. All of this is directed towards letting parents know that what they do and think is crucial to their child's learning.

 What is your school doing with pre-school children and their parents? Make a list. What activities would you add to your list? Where would you start on your additions? What organisational arrangements need to be made?

Let's move on into the classroom, thinking about children as they come to school. Most of them are eager to learn how to read. You yourself want to move away from a highly structured reading scheme, but you have been used to having this support in the initial stages. If you take this aid away — perhaps by putting the readers in the book corner where children can take them if they want to — what will you put in their place? It's not a straight substitution of one kind of book for another because there are many other learning activities that are interwoven into a whole approach. Nevertheless, a shortlist of books that you could work with might be a good place to start.

CHOOSING BOOKS FOR BEGINNER READERS

These are the books that you would share with the whole class, reading them more than once so that they become familiar. Children would then read their choices on their own, take them home or share them with a friend. They would bring to the books what Frank Smith calls 'non-visual information'. They would know a lot about the book they choose and may even have most of it off by heart. Teachers who work in this way usually have about 20 books as their introduction to reading.

You might put this group of books on tape so that children have the added support and interest of hearing as they read. They might take the tape-book set home to share with parents or brothers and sisters.

You and the children might choose some of these books as the basis for drawing and writing activities. This might lead to making class books which carry through on the theme or which originate further adventures of the characters.

It would undoubtedly be useful to have some criteria for selecting your small collection of good books for the first few weeks in the reception class. Here are some of the things to look out for:

- It is enjoyable to the readers — children first, then teachers and other adult helpers.
- It is highly predictable.
- It has a strong story line.
- It repeats patterns of story and language.
- It has a cumulative pattern of story and language.
- It has lively, interesting illustrations that add to or help tell the story.
- It has stories or rhymes that children are already familiar with.
- It has rhyme or a rhythm.
- It is easy to join in with.
- It has humour.
- It sounds good when read aloud.
- It wears well on rereading and can be talked about more than once.
- It has a good, clear layout.
- It is not too long.

see ref. 10 Jill Bennett's book *Learning to read with picture books* is a good point of reference on selection criteria. See also the appendix for a suggested short list of titles.

1 hour

Bring together six books that you like to read with beginner readers. Look at the criteria suggested above. Do your books match up to the criteria? Would you change or add to the suggested list of criteria?

The first criterion in the list is that a book is enjoyable for you and the children. So you need to find time to read for yourself, as well as talk to other teachers, children and parents about books they have enjoyed. The big format books that are now being published with sets of small books are ideal for a group, or even for a whole class, to read and talk about. These big format books give you the advantage of being able to run your finger along the text as you read, to help children make the connection between the spoken and written word. Children can join in with some of the reading and, of course, the pictures are large and clear enough for everyone to see them easily. Later in the reading process you can also use these books with groups of children to identify individual words. The sets of normal-sized books which come with them can be used for group reading and talking and individual books can be taken home to share with parents.

see ref. 11 *Better move on, Frog* by Ron Maris is an ideal book for beginner readers. It is simple but interesting with beautiful, clear illustrations that help to tell the story and give an added sophistication at the end. The story begins with a homeless frog who is looking for somewhere to live. It is confronted by lots of holes, the habitats of creatures it meets as the story goes on.

The refrain "Better move on, Frog, this hole is full of..." is carried through the story as the frog sees only a pair of eyes at first. The owners are identified on the subsequent page. As the story goes along, the various creatures who have already been identified — rabbits, badgers, bees, mice — join the frog in the quest for a home. This is shown in lively illustrations.

At last Frog finds an empty hole, which is a garden pond. The refrain changes to "But look — better move in, Frog, and wait for the hole to fill up."

There is a happy ending when Frog meets up with another frog. It then begins to rain. The friendly animals return to their own homes, the pond fills up and the two frogs settle in. The last picture shows lots of baby frogs playing on lily pads.

The aim of a collection of beginner books is to give children a platform of familiar and well-liked books that they can build on with confidence. You, parents and other experienced readers also help them to extend their reading horizons by reading with them books that they want to read yet cannot tackle independently.

Many of these early books have a structure or, more precisely, a pattern and shape that make them predictable and give children confidence and enjoyment. It is a very different structure from some early readers that rely foremost on repetition of individual words in such a way that makes the reading dull and flat. The language is sometimes so contrived that it is difficult to read, being unlike both the spoken and the storybook language with which children are familiar. It belongs in a wasteland of reading schemes that children have to struggle to master, and then later relinquish when they read more widely. The contrived language and content can make it very difficult for children to predict — and prediction or good guessing is the child's most powerful learning strategy. If this is weakened, then the child is thrown back on configuration and sound-to-letter correspondence only.

The same argument applies to children for whom English is a second language, and who are becoming bilingual. They need to build from their experience of spoken language by reading and writing it, and to build on their experience of listening and responding to story and rhyme by reading it.

In an approach to reading which seems natural, the child and adult reader will reread the text many times with satisfaction and enjoyment. This is part of what we might call 'readerly behaviour'. This is how readers read — revisiting texts that give them pleasure. It would be difficult to apply this to some of the early readers in reading schemes.

Children who are restricted to these talk about finishing a book and getting on to the next one. It is difficult to imagine them revisiting these texts. This would mean going backwards in a graded structure, with implications of failure in their own eyes and in the eyes of their friends and parents.

So, before the children come to you, or as a first step in a different approach, you could select and get books of the sort that meet our criteria. The text is vital, because we learn something about reading each time we open a book. There must be enjoyment, satisfaction and meaning for children from the start. If their first books at school give them this, they are more likely to become lifelong readers.

READING TOGETHER ONE TO ONE

Reading together, teacher and child, is still at the heart of learning to read. This shared activity, so central to reading, is not only important as a learning process. The value of undivided attention from a trusted adult cannot be over-estimated.

Parents can read with their child in the same way, especially if they are guided and advised by teachers and if there is a continuing dialogue between parent and teacher. Children who read regularly with their parents within an organised home-school reading programme often say how much they value having a parent to themselves. In the appendix there is a short list of books and booklets available to help teachers in setting up and sustaining home-school reading programmes.

WHAT HAPPENS WHEN TEACHER AND CHILD READ TOGETHER

To start reading together, sometimes the child chooses the book and sometimes the child and you choose it together. Most often it will be a book which the child can join in with to a fair degree. At this early stage, it will also usually be a book that can be read at one sitting.

The emphasis is on sharing the reading with the child rather than just listening to the child read. You and the child talk around the book, discussing the title and the pictures,

and speculating on what might happen in the story. You might start the reading, pausing for the child to predict, join in, reflect on the story or the pictures. After the story is finished, the child might go back and look at particular words or phrases, and then read some of the story. The child's turn at reading might be saved for another time, or the book might be taken home that evening. You might talk about what the child has enjoyed in this book and might enjoy reading next. You might then make some kind of record of the activity.

Many teachers prefer having one longer reading session once or twice a week than the daily few moments, which seem rushed and distracted. In the frantic scramble to try to hear everyone read every day, it is difficult to get into a story and talk about it. It can all start to resemble a production line, with children waiting, children reading and a beleaguered teacher in between trying to get through the statutory two pages as quickly as possible. Besides there are other people who can read with children and other valuable reading experiences that do not make children so dependent on the teacher.

The teachers who answered our questionnaire were sure

of the importance of reading to children, even if they didn't manage to do it as often as they intended. Reading to a class can give children enjoyment, satisfaction, a chance to share their responses and ideas, an opportunity to empathise with characters, to compare their experiences, to laugh or cry together, to wriggle with suspense. When listening to you read, children also learn how to talk about books and reading. They learn the basic vocabulary of dealing with books — 'page', 'cover', 'word', 'letter'. Gradually they learn the vocabulary for discussing books — 'character', 'plot', 'style'.

Because there is such a vast range of good and exciting books for children, reading to a class can widen their experience of genre, of different writers, of technique. This is especially important for children who make a slow start or who do not readily and immediately turn to books as a source of satisfaction and pleasure.

READING AND WRITING GO TOGETHER

Some of the early reading of young children will be from their own writing. At their earliest stages, children will

105

sometimes compose while you or another adult transcribes. Composer and scribe will then read the story together, perhaps many times. This way of working reinforces the reading and the writing processes.

As young children develop, they will share their writing with other children in the class. Donald Graves and others have brought the writing process into focus in the primary school. The *National writing project newsletter* and *Language matters*, published at CLPE, are full of examples of successful practice giving glimpses into lively and interesting writing with young children. Infant teachers are renowned for their ingenuity and originality in helping children write and make books. Time is probably the only limiting factor.

see ref. 12

see ref. 13

see ref. 14

In some schools, parents and other community members help with the reading and writing process, and children are motivated to raise their performance as writers and readers. Some of the LEA projects within the National Writing Project focused on this kind of shared writing. The booklets produced from these ventures are fascinating and inspiring to read. In the Family Books Project in Lambeth, London, parents write a book for their own child and the teacher helps illustrate and produce it. If it has been written in the home language, the teacher also finds a way to make an English version available.

Sometimes the teacher and the whole class write a book together. This might arise from an outing they went on, or perhaps from a book that had been read to the class. One reception class which had enjoyed Pat Hutchins' *Rosie's walk* many times began collecting red things. They went on a 'red' walk with the teacher, taking polaroid photos of everything of that colour around the school neighbourhood. The photos became the illustrations for a class book composed by the children and transcribed by the teacher, originally onto large sheets of kitchen paper so that they could all see her writing. The language style might have owed a lot to the author, but it was their own work — and the book was instantly readable by most of the children.

see ref. 15

Another class, many of whose members used English as a second language, had developed many class books. The stories had been taped to help children with listening comprehension. Their latest book was a monster fantasy called *Nottiberky* (see pages 108–113). The process of making this book is interesting and informative, though it owes a lot to the particular teacher's skill and ingenuity. The steps were as follows:

1 The idea of the plot was a monster who ate words.

2 The children composed the first draft, which was written by the class teacher on a large sheet of paper with the children watching.

3 The draft was read together and altered by the teacher at the children's suggestion.

4 The school secretary typed the final copy on A4 paper.

5 The text was duplicated with one copy for each child, one for the class library, one for the school library, extras for visitors.

6 Children worked on their own copy, adding dialogue in speech bubbles, illustrations and extras, and then took it home.

A shared book can be the basis of reading and writing at any stage. A class of six- to seven-year-olds had heard some of the 'Clever Polly and the stupid wolf' stories and had revelled in them. Some of the children chose to write more adventures for the two characters, working in pairs. Little books were produced and added to the books in the reading corner — they looked attractive and were always in demand. One group went further and wanted to write a play. They had to understand the format for playwriting and this did not take them long to acquire. With the help of one of the parents who helped in the class regularly, the playlet was typed up, parts were distributed and learned and finally the play was performed for the rest of the class. Copies of the play were kept in the book corner and small groups read it together, taking the parts.

The word processor has its part to play in all this with programmes enabling simple editing. It is commonplace to see quite young children working together at a word processor. Watching them, we can see clearly how listening, talking, reading and writing interrelate.

Notti berky

The Nottiberky came from the planet Zerdz. His favourite
thing was eating WORDS! The Nottiberky would munch a pile of
words for his lunch, and without a plate of words for dinner,
the Nottiberky got much thinner. You always knew where he had
been, not one word could be seen!

One day in Cranford Infant School he found millions and
millions of words all around. "Aaaaah!" he cried, "This is
the place I see, where I can live quite happily." At once he
began to eat words from the books and from the walls, from the
corridor and the door; even from clothes the children wore!
Soon all the words were gone; he hadn't left a single one!

Well, you can guess - we were in a mess!

All the children and teachers were sad. It really was very
bad.   What could be done to get words once more, in books, on
walls, in the corridor, and on the clothes the children wore.
At last Navdeep had a good idea.   "Let's make him mad, then he
will shout and all the words will come back out."   So all the
children called him nasty names, pulled his tail and played
bad games.. The Nottiberky went red with rage and yelled out
loudly with a shout, "STOP IT" - then all the words came
tumbling out!

The Nottiberky said "You don't like me, so I'll go back home
for tea."

Now we are happy, once again, Cranford Infant's is the same.
There are millions and millions of words to be found. They
are everywhere – all around – and we like reading them.

LISTENING-AND-READING TAPES

A collection of listening-and-reading tapes in the classroom is invaluable. With a junction box and headphones, children can take advantage of them during busy times in the classroom or during quiet times set aside for reading. Since the children themselves control the operation, they can listen as many times as they like. The tapes can include the books that most of the children can read independently, and books and poems that extend the children's reading repertoire. Children often join in with the tape — this is also especially helpful for children with English as a second language.

THE BOOK CORNER

The book corner, comfortable with cushions on the floor and bright with books, is the best place to be in many classrooms. Partly secluded and well lit, it is inviting and easily associated with pleasure and comfort. The selection of books needs to cater for all tastes and include non-fiction books. The books that you have read with the class might be located together so that children who aren't yet wide readers know there are books they can manage.

Sometimes an overlarge selection can be confusing, so it might be better to keep some books in reserve and make an occasional change. It's also a good idea to swap part of the class collection with another class. This makes the collection more interesting and the money goes further.

Although hardback books are more expensive, it's good to have a selection of these — they look and feel quite different from paperbacks and, of course, last longer. If you have parents, other adults or older children reading with young children, they could sometimes just sit in the book corner, ready and willing to talk and read with whoever is there.

It's good to have groups of children helping you to maintain the book corner and mount displays. If everyone in turns takes responsibility and the book corner is well maintained, children get the idea that books are of worth, and will care for them.

The book corner is a good place to read with a friend.

114

Every class has more experienced readers who enjoy reading to less experienced readers. Where there is no graded scheme, children are less competitive about finishing one book and going on to the next. In this more relaxed atmosphere, children learn a lot from sharing their reading.

THE NEED TO READ

Most of this chapter has been about reading books, but there are other kinds of reading. For example, urgent reading is concerned with the need to understand and perhaps respond immediately to a written communicatioon. There are many opportunities for this kind of reading in your classroom and school. Here is a starter list:

- Messages, notices, reminders, announcements, instructions on the blackboard, on notice boards, on the door, anywhere. "Whose turn is it to take the gerbils home?" "Remind me to give out the letters at home time." "We have an extra PE session tomorrow, so remember your kit." "We are having storytime with Class 3 today." "Peter's mum had a baby girl today; her name is Jenny." "Please come in quietly, we are all reading."
- Personal notes and messages.
- Menus.
- Labels.
- Checklists of activities completed or attempted.
- Charts for keeping observations and for working from.
- Captions on displays that pose genuine questions.

Urgent reading which evokes a response is an important part of children's learning inside and outside school.

THE 'LITERATE HOME-CORNER'

see ref. 16 In his book *The emergence of literacy*, Nigel Hall writes about promoting literacy within the home-corner and the interesting effects this has on children's reading and writing. The literate home-corner includes the *Radio Times*, *TV Times*, directories, magazines, a reminder board, pads and writing implements by the telephone and with the shopping basket.

PEOPLE WHO CAN HELP

Thankfully the class teacher isn't the only person who can help children learn to read. Parents, other adults and other children, particularly older children, can all take a part. They are 'members of The Literacy Club' to which young, inexperienced readers can be apprenticed.

Many teachers arrange for older and younger children to share books and read together regularly. In one such arrangement, junior children not only shared the books that were in the infant classroom but brought a book of their choice with them. Junior and infant class teachers attest to the fact that it works well for both sides of the partnership, and is particularly valuable for giving older, less sure readers boost. Links like this have sometimes been the foundation of closer working between infant and junior schools that share the same site.

Parents' potential contribution to their child's reading has been mentioned earlier in the chapter. They are often invited into the classroom to share in children's reading. One successful practice is to ask parents to come in at nine o'clock at the beginning of school to share in the daily quiet reading time for half an hour. In this way, parents not only share books with their own children, but can read with a group and help in choosing books as well.

Although this chapter has focused mainly on the classroom, children's reading can also be developed and promoted within the larger school community. Some schools have regular 'book assemblies' in which children and teachers read extracts from favourite books. Some schools hold a 'book week' every year with a varied programme of events including the visits of writers. Some schools run a bookshop, often with the help of parents, on the theory that owning books is important if children are going to be lifelong readers.

The school library is an important place, giving children a wider choice of reading and a different environment in which to enjoy books. Sometimes parents help in maintaining the library. Lively focus displays are mounted and children are guided into library use. Often teachers make links between the school and the public library. Visits to the local library are made and children are encouraged to join as regular members and to participate in events held during school holidays.

SUMMARY

This chapter has been about some of the practical ways in which you, the class teacher, can help children learn to read. The suggestions come from working with and learning from class teachers and children who are not relying on graded and structured materials for their reading. The suggestions include how parents can be encouraged to participate in the reading process. Because reading cannot be seen in isolation, ways have been suggested in which reading and writing, talking and listening all work together. Attention has been given to the value of having an experienced reader, whether an older child or an adult, share a book with an inexperienced reader. The web of learning to read has many threads, but the young child is its vital centre.

We can see that there are really three 'teachers' of reading: the text, the experienced reader and the children with their understanding of the world and of stories.

Perhaps the last word should be from the probationary teacher who said, "Once you decide upon reading without schemes, there's no end to the things you think of doing!"

Chapter 7

HOW DO YOU KNOW IT'S WORKING?

So now you have revised your approach.

How do you know it's working?

How do you know it's better?

How do you know it's setting children on the way to becoming independent and committed readers?

In answering these important questions, we first look at the options commonly used for monitoring and assessing children's individual development in reading. Then we discuss what benefits we are hoping for in the wider picture.

In any area of learning and teaching, we need to try to evaluate, monitor and assess what is going on. This is especially true if we are developing new ideas and approaches. It is needed in order to:

- give ourselves a clearer picture of children's development;
- assure ourselves of children's continuing growth;
- reflect on how we could accelerate or consolidate areas of growth and identify areas of weakness;
- communicate children's progress to other agents in children's learning;
- explain and justify our thinking and practice;
- modify and develop further our teaching approaches.

There are many different ways in which we can express and record what we see to be development and growth.

STANDARDISED READING TESTS

Standardised tests are normative, that is, they give a reading age or quotient as a measurement. This enables us to compare one child's performance against another's and all our children against national norms. Some tests also have a diagnostic element which helps expose areas of weakness.

see ref. 17 In 1983 Caroline Gipps wrote that 70% of LEAs carried out standardised reading tests, most often when children were moving from one phase of schooling to another. The Young's Group Reading Test, in which pictures and words are matched and sentences completed, was at that time very popular. It was inexpensive and easy to administer.

Standardised reading tests come in many shapes and sizes. These include:

- word recognition tests — children read aloud a sheet of unrelated words that are graded for difficulty;
- picture-word matching tests;
- sentence completion tests — words to complete usually unconnected sentences are often given in multiple choice;
- continuous passages — these are read aloud or silently, sometimes followed by questions;
- cloze texts — blanks are left for words to be written in.

There are some difficulties with standardised reading tests. Most are based on a linear concept in which one small skill is built on another. Development in any aspect of language is not linear. There can be leaps forward, pauses on a plateau, regressions.

The *Bullock report* recommends that we do not use any tests more than 10 years old, yet many in current use are much older. Language changes; tests date; norms have to be re-established as standards of literacy alter.

see ref. 18 Look at these sentences from the Daniels and Diack Test of Reading Competence. Are they still relevant today?

Men's socks are usually (matter/stolen/wasted/knitted).

A steam engine usually runs on (rails/reels/stoves/signals).

A place where talking films are shown is called a (theatre/cinema/gallery/house).

The context of testing is also problematical. Who will administer the test and in what situation? If the head does it on behalf of the busy class teacher, children may feel more nervous and anxious. Indeed, however the situation is disguised, children usually realise they are being tested.

The reading task performed in the test is unrelated to what is going on in the class and to the various kinds of reading that the child chooses. It has no meaning for the child. It just measures a child's performance in one reading task on one day.

It seems unlikely that the complex web of behaviour, understanding and attitudes we are hoping children will develop is open to measurement by most of the reading tests in common use.

There is also a danger of relying too much on the outcomes of standardised tests in judging whether a project has worked or not.

see ref. 19 In the Belfield Reading Project, for instance, there were no significant gains in standardised test scores at the end of a period in which parents were involved in reading with their children. Everyone knew that the children were profiting from the experience, but for a while some teachers wavered. They were temporarily swayed by the scores on reading tests to doubt the evidence of their own eyes.

CRITERION-REFERENCED TESTS

These tests are designed to show what a child can do within a set reading task or within a series of tasks. The Assessment of Performance Unit used criterion-referenced tests in their survey of schools. Teachers can devise or choose their own texts for children to read aloud, read silently and answer questions about.

INFORMAL READING INVENTORIES

Informal reading inventories, usually in the form of a chart or a checklist, can show the kinds of reading strategies that children use. To help compile a reading inventory, teachers might use cloze texts or a form of miscue analysis as well as various kinds of observations.

PROFILING

Profiles give a rounded picture, and schools more and more are looking to this method. A reading profile would almost certainly be part of a whole language profile encompassing listening, talking and writing as well. It would be made up of a series of 'staging points' in a child's growth towards becoming an independent, committed reader. Profiles would include a record of the child's preferences in and attitudes towards reading. Children, parents and teachers would all contribute to the profile, which would serve as a working record and as information to be transferred to other people concerned with children's reading.

see ref. 20   In her book *Read with me*, Liz Waterland suggests a circular 'reading behaviour record' which many teachers have taken up and found useful and illuminating.

This kind of record shows understanding gained as children become more experienced readers and reflects observations of children while they are sharing reading with the teacher and when they are reading independently.

The record includes observations on how willingly children come to read and how they listen to stories, right through to reading widely and independently.

The underlying principle of profiles is the 'observable behaviour' of children. There are particularly fruitful times for teachers and other adults to observe children. These include:

- when children are in the book corner;
- when teachers and children read together;
- when everyone is settled with a book during a quiet time;
- when the teacher or other adult is reading to a group.

Perhaps the most favourable time for observation is when a child and a teacher read together. Sometimes it's good to make a tape-recording of the session. This gives you the opportunity to reflect on the reading later when listening to the tape.

Whatever kinds of record we are going to keep, parents and children need to contribute to them. We have to bear three principles in mind about records:

1 The compiling of the record must not take too long.
2 The record must be informative.
3 The record must be read and used to guide further action.

Most LEAs have guidelines for compiling records. These can be a starting point, but it is a very valuable exercise for teachers in a school to get together and formulate their own particular system. The discussion itself is an important learning process and should not be underestimated.

Having thought about observing and recording the individual reader's development, let's move on to a wider view of the kinds of benefits we are hoping that children will gain from a revised approach to reading.

We would like to consider this area first in terms of what happens initially in infant classrooms, and then in terms of the effects on the older reader in the junior school. Our work must be seen as a long-term aim to help children become not only fluent readers, but keen and motivated to read the rest of their lives. Concern that they do well in the annual reading test becomes less important.

WITHIN A TERM

"The whole atmosphere in the school changed overnight." This dramatic statement was made about the effect of widening the reading materials available and allowing the children to choose their own. It came from the head teacher of a large infant school in Barrow.

The sorts of things to which she was referring exactly fit the list made by Carol Green, whose encouragement to parents to keep a personal record of their children's progress resulted in the reports quoted on pages 25 to 28. Carol Green herself kept a record of two terms in which she made the break from reading schemes and sought involvement from the parents. Under the heading of 'Positive things which seem to be happening in reading', she listed:

1 The children enjoy reading more than in former years.
2 The adults enjoy hearing children read.
3 The children see themselves as readers. There are no children who clearly see themselves as failures, but in previous years a few would have done. The children tell me they can read; they treat each other as readers.
4 More children are reading to their peers.
5 The volume of reading has increased enormously.
6 The care of books has improved.
7 More children turn to books when they have a choice.

These observations are echoed over and over by other teachers who have decided to develop their practice in the ways we have described.

ENTHUSIASM OF TEACHERS AND CHILDREN

Teaching is all about generating enthusiasm, which is the great motivator for achievement. A teacher should create and sustain enthusiasm, and the best way to do this is by being enthusiastic yourself. When both teachers and children enjoy the reading and share the delights, learning will occur naturally. This implies that the books available for reading are worth reading. It is difficult to get excited by some of the characters and books in some popular reading schemes.

On one occasion an infant teacher played us a tape of herself hearing a five-year-old read his latest book from the reading scheme. She sounded desperate to get some excitement into her voice when talking about the character getting up, going on the bus, meeting his friends, going home and getting back into bed. As she listened, she began to smile, and soon we were all laughing together. Finally she exclaimed, "It's all very well to laugh, but you try sounding excited by that book!"

Certainly there was little indication that the child felt inspired to put drama into his reading. His voice was a slow, steady drone lacking spark of any kind. Clearly he was reading this book to prove he could say the words right and get through it. The quality of a book's text and illustrations will determine whether children develop as readers, becoming excited, at times spellbound, by reading.

READING BY CHOICE MEANS READING MORE

Recently one of us was invited by a local infant school to work one day a week for a term with the reception teacher and three volunteer students from Charlotte Mason College. The aim of the project was to create an environment and develop activities which would motivate children to want to read. We called it 'The need to read'. The teacher used a core reading scheme, *One, two, three and away*, supplemented by some *Story chest* books which at first were kept on a shelf out of the children's reach. In addition, there were two book racks containing some picture books from the county library van.

On their arrival at school, children were free to choose an activity. It was noticeable that few if any chose to read. So, as a first step in our project, we decided to borrow 60 picture books from the schools library service and create a cosy corner in which they could be read. We wrote to parents asking for any cushions they could spare. In fact, a group of children composed the letter as part of the project and the teacher wrote it with a thick felt-tipped pen on white sugar paper. The following morning, the reading corner was scattered with cushions!

At first few children ventured into it. The teacher and others sat there ready to share books with the children. It took a number of mornings before children favoured it. After a few weeks, though, children quite naturally were making for it and curling up to read individually or in pairs. There is no doubt that the volume of reading increased dramatically, and that the whole attitude of the children to reading and books became much more positive.

BEHAVING AND THINKING AS A READER

Reading is a natural and necessary activity. We are surrounded by print every day and we respond to it, following signs, looking at labels, snatching the words of an advertisement. For most of us, reading lengthy texts is just as natural: newspapers, magazines, books. Give us an interesting text and we immediately behave as natural readers. By keeping books away from children, out of reach, to be dispensed only by the teacher, we prevent children from developing 'readerly' behaviour. Reading becomes something which is only done on particular occasions, when teacher says so. Children become passive readers, simply waiting for their turn. The sort of teaching strategies we are advocating in this book encourage children to think of themselves as readers even before they can read a word!

The book corner described is just such an encouragement. Children could be seen browsing through the books, trying to decide which they might like. A book would be picked up, the cover studied intently, perhaps a few pages flicked over, and then rejected, for reasons known only to the child. Another would then be tried and, for whatever reason, be chosen. Exactly the same behaviour by adults can be seen in any library and bookshop in the country, but with one important difference. Whereas an adult's choice becomes the 'reading book', the children's choice in the book corner was an 'extra'. The book from which the child learned to read was still provided by the teacher. The teacher began to appreciate that children's perception of learning to read could be distorted if they have a 'reading book' and other books. This awareness began the process of the school examining its approach to reading.

Encouraging children to think of themselves as readers and behave as such means that learning to read in classrooms reflects reading in the world outside. The developing ability of the child to make choices, with the teacher in a subtle advisory role, is evidence of success. When the book corner is well populated and more children are keen to choose and share books with interested adults, we are succeeding. We are enabling children to develop into lifelong readers.

The child's perspective The quotations from children on pages 45 to 49 provide a fascinating window on the way they view reading and the business of learning to read. On a reading scheme, success and failure are easily worked out: "If I'm on book 10, I must be a better reader than my friend who is only on book eight." "If I am allowed to read books from the orange box, then I am not as good as those who choose from the red box." For the vast majority of children, the race through the reading scheme or colour boxes is an indication of success. For some the initial failure to make headway is devastating. Within a few weeks of arrival at school they are struggling, bringing up the rear in the race through the reading books. Before too long they do not see themselves as successful learners and readers.

In contrast, think of children with a wide variety of unnumbered and uncoloured books, available for all to share with teachers, parents, older children. The books simply *see ref. 21* become 'popular' and 'less popular'. A child choosing *Spot's first walk* will not be adversely compared to the child who *see ref. 22* chooses *Not now, Bernard!* Both books will be thought of as 'good' by the whole class. Both readers will have status. The minimising of children's perceptions of themselves as successes or failures so early on in their lives must be a major advantage of the approaches we advocate. Reading then develops not as a race to the end of the scheme, but through the power of the books themselves. It is the *experience* of reading which will produce children who want to read, can read, and do read.

WRITING

Reading and writing should develop together as complementary parts of the same process. Reading presents us with models of how to write: we could not write a newspaper article if we had never read a newspaper. The ability of children to compose comes before they can actually write, but this ability will depend on the sorts of books they read. A narrow diet — at worst, one reading scheme — presents an extremely limited model of what we can do with writing. The stilted prose of many early readers gives rise to the stilted first attempts at writing of many infants.

We would argue that, while the development of transcription skills (of which handwriting is the most important in the early stages) must be a major strategy of infant teachers, children must also be encouraged to compose lengthy pieces. This can be done in two ways, both of which can become a natural feature of life in the classroom. First, you can act as the scribe for a child or a group of children and write down what they compose: stories, instructions, letters home, whatever else. (You may recall that the letter asking parents for cushions for the reading corner of one school was produced like this.) Whenever we do this, we realise just what five-year-olds can do. A child who is able to compose a story which reads like a story is well on the way to becoming a reader. This ability is another measure of success of what we are trying to do for reading.

Secondly, reading aloud from books written in richly different ways exposes children to the finest use of language. This helps them to develop an awareness of what written language sounds like and what writers can do with it.

INTO THE JUNIORS

The need for children to learn how to read a wide variety of books in the infant school is plain to see when we consider 9-, 10- and 11-year-olds trying to read novels and reference materials. A narrow diet from ages five to nine will mean that children will not have developed the reading awareness and reading skills necessary to cope with more complex books. Unfortunately, it is the fate of many juniors as well to be fed poorly. Most of the infant schemes carry on into the junior classroom. Yet the longer children are kept on the structured scheme, the greater the gap which develops between them and the world of literature.

The sorts of books which develop reading skills and habits are readily available and can be found on the shelves of any bookshop or library. We are in a golden age of junior fiction, with many superb writers producing novels and poetry. Alan Garner, Leon Garfield, Betsy Byars, Nina Bawden — these are just some of the names on a very long list. We find it incomprehensible that a 10-year-old should be reading book 87 of some scheme when, at that moment, it would be *see ref. 23* possible to be entering the magical world of *The iron man* *see ref. 24* (Ted Hughes), *The snow spider* (Jenny Nimmo) or *Goodnight* *see ref. 25* *Mr Tom* (Michelle Magorian).

The novels mentioned offer a marked contrast to junior scheme books in a number of ways, all of which form part of what we mean by success or failure of reading in school. First and most obviously, they are much longer. This helps children develop the stamina and ability for sustained reading and tunes them into the subtle development of plot and character only possible in longer works. Even the most advanced scheme books are relatively short, often further split into short stories. Characters in short stories do not develop because there is neither time nor space to do so. This gives rise to the child reader who complains of being bored by many novels because "nothing happens" quickly enough. They have been raised on a pap diet of quick, easy stories and are not able to appreciate the richness and nourishment of a full-blown novel.

Secondly, the language in scheme books is usually limited in vocabulary, lacking sweep and breadth. In contrast, here see ref. 26 is an extract from *The wolves of Willoughby Chase*. (Ten-year-old Sylvia has arrived, exhausted, to stay with her cousin Bonnie, at Willoughby Chase.)

...and a kindly voice (that of Pattern, the maid) saying "Poor little dear, she is wearied to death. James, do you take her upstairs while I ask Mrs Shubunkin for a posset."

The posset came, steaming, sweet, and delicious, and Pattern's gentle hands removed Sylvia's travelling clothes. Sylvia was too sleepy to study her surroundings before she was placed between soft, smooth sheets and sank into dreamless slumber.

Later in the night she awoke, and saw stars shining beyond the white curtain at her bed's foot. Suddenly she recalled Aunt Jane's voice teaching her astronomy: "There is Orion, Sylvia dear, and the constellation resembling a W is Cassiopeia." Oh, poor Aunt Jane! Would she be lying awake too, watching the stars? Would she be warm enough under the jet-trimmed mantle? What would she do at breakfast-time with no niece to warm the teapot, brew the Bohea, and make the toast-gruel?

Joan Aiken has written of her problems with American publishers who wanted her to simplify and modernise her prose because, they said, American children would not be able to understand it. This is exactly the same argument which determines the anaemic style of vocabulary of junior reading schemes. And what an empty argument it is! One which totally fails to appreciate how and why we read fiction! Through her use of words and phrases now only part of the history of our language, Joan Aiken charms the reader into the world she is creating. It does not matter one bit that children might have only a hazy notion of the meaning of 'posset' or 'jet-trimmed mantle' or 'Bohea' or 'toast-gruel'. What these words do is reek of atmosphere. No need to rush immediately to the dictionary to discover their exact meanings. Rather, we soak up their sounds and evocations, allowing them to build up the sense of time past in which the plot unfolds. Can you imagine possets and Boheas in a reading scheme?

The third limitation in the junior scheme is due to a combination of short length and an overriding concern with simple language and structure, as already discussed. Before explaining this further, let's look at this extract from Alan *see ref. 27* Garner's marvellous fantasy, *The weirdstone of Brisingamen.* (At this point, the children and their companions are trying to keep themselves hidden from evil birds.)

"The lodge was bad," said Susan, "but after the strain of that drive I nearly collapsed when we had to walk out in full view of the big house and all those staring windows."

"*We* had to drop flat twice in front of the house!" said Colin. "If anyone was watching, they must have thought we were mad."

"Ay, it was a bit strenuous," said Gowther. "How do you think we fared?"

"The birds missed us, I think," said Fenodyree, "and I saw no one in the rooms. How was it with you, cousin?"

"I saw no one, and heard naught: we have done well."

But garrulous old Jim Trafford was a small man, and it was his afternoon off. By half past two he was in his accustomed corner in the Harrington Arms, and monopolizing the conversation of four of his acquaintances.

"I reckon it's twice as cowd as it were eleven year back," he said. "I've seen nowt like it; it's enough fer t'send you mazed. Eh, and I think it's takken one or two like that round 'ere this morning. No, listen! It were nobbut a couple of hours since, nawther. I were up at th'all, going round seeing as they were orreet fer coal afore I come away, and one o'th'fires were low, like, so I gets down fer

129

t'give it a poke. Well, I'm straightening up again, and I 'appens fer t'look out o' th'winder, and what does I see? I'll tell yer. Theer was two little fellers, about so 'igh, gooing past th' 'ouse towards Pyethorne. No listen! They wore white capes wi' 'oods as come over their faces, and they kept peering round, and up, and down, and walking 'alf back'ards. I'll swear as one 'em 'ad a beard—a yeller un it were. It's th' gospel truth!

"Well, I shakes me 'ead, and carries me bucket into th' next room. Fire's orreet theer, but scuttle wants a lump or two. On me way out I looks through th' winder, and theer they are again! And this time I sees a good bit o' beard, but now it's black!

"Round and round they scowls, then they drops flat on their faces, and pull their 'eads and legs in like tortoises. It's a fact! You conner 'ardly see 'em agen th' snow. Well, after a minute two, they gets up, and off they trots, back to back now, if you please! Then smack on their faces again! I tell yer, I couldner 'ardly credit it. I watches them while they're near to th' wood, then they puts down their 'eads, and runs! It's this 'ere frost what's be'ind it, and no error. Theer'll be a few like them, I'll tell thee, if we 'ave much more o' this…. Eh, Fred! What's to do? Art feeling ill? What's th' 'urry?"

The door slammed.

"Eh, what's up wi' 'im? Eh, you lot, come over 'ere!"

One parent described what happened when he was reading this part of the novel aloud to his 10-year-old son. The child was confused by the sudden switch in focus from the children to a new character in a pub. He couldn't work out what was going on, asking such questions as, "Who is he?", "Is he telling the children?", "Which pub?" Experienced readers immediately recognise the common device in fiction of a sudden change of scene and the use of a character simply to further the plot. We accept that connections will be made and simply wait for the author to make things clear. But we have learned about this technique only from reading other novels. We have built up literary competence, the reading of one novel helping us to read the next.

Unless children are reading a wide variety of fiction from their earliest encounters with picture books, they will not be able to develop this literary competence. The great thing is that many contemporary picture books for young readers are extremely sophisticated, and facilitate this development. So, see ref. 28 in *Rosie's walk*, children learn about a reader's relationship see ref. 29 with the writer, for both know more than Rosie. In *Where the wild things are* (Maurice Sendak), they learn to interpret from see ref. 30 clues in the text and pictures. In *Come away from the water, Shirley* (John Burningham), they learn to make connections as complex as those in the extract quoted above. What these books all have in common is the way they induce the reader's active involvement with the text, including interpretations. This is a far cry from the expressed aims of reading schemes, and yet is vital if we want to produce children who can read in the junior school.

As the above arguments indicate, we judge the success of our approach to reading on a very different set of criteria than a score in a reading test. The aim of the teacher becomes primarily to motivate children through the shared reading of mind-stretching books. Through such reading, the child learns just what it is that readers have to do. Each book read from ages five to 11 will be a pleasant, unselfconscious reading lesson, the text itself demonstrating just how it has to be read, the teacher acting as a trusted guide. Each book read adds to the literary competence of the child, and new words are learned because of the way they tell the story. Such reading lessons will take place at home as well as at school, with parents, nans, grandads, brothers, sisters, friends. They will produce children who not only can read in the narrow sense of recognising words, but who are able also to enter the world of imaginative writing at its best — and who want to do so.

Assess some children as readers: use either our suggestions or ideas of your own.
- Note down what you have learned.
- Reflect on what you still do not know.
- Discuss with colleagues how you could make a better assessment.

NOW AND THEN

You will want to repeat this TIME OUT at future stages of the development to evaluate progress. It is a TIME OUT for now and a TIME OUT for then.

You have read this far through the book and discussed with each other ways in which you would like to develop your approach, as a school, to helping children learn to read.

You will have fairly definite ideas of what sorts of practice you are actually going to adopt.

You will have thought through the challenges associated with the development and you will be prepared to address the difficulties that arise.

You will be clear about the sorts of outcomes that will follow your new development in the ways children will approach and conduct themselves as readers.

There is one more thing that you must do. You must give yourself the chance to evaluate your new approach. While it takes a little time at the beginning, it will prove its worth later. Remember, you need a clear picture of your starting point so that you will know whether there have been real developments and growth within the terms you see as important.

If we say that an approach to reading which allows children choice and encourages understanding and real readership will lead to certain outcomes, we need to measure the outcomes to check our effectiveness. We cannot rely on intuition only.

This TIME OUT encourages you to re-examine the current situation in the classroom. To look at your own situation can be useful and enjoyable, and can increase your fascination with the teaching and learning world.

We want to take some samples of the sorts of activity which we predict will be enhanced by developing our approach to helping children learn to read.

If we record now and in six, 12 and 18 months' time, we will have a set of figures which will show realistically whether the approach has been worthwhile. We will be able to look at development factually rather than playing hunches or using extremes of success or failure to prove our points. Above all our recording of data will help us to keep clear in our mind the reasons for adopting the approach.

The record tries to quantify parts of classroom practice. It may be that you would wish to do it, but teaching and recording on the hoof are not the easiest things to do. Maybe this is the opportunity to present real situations in mathematics to older children in the primary school. Perhaps this is the chance to involve parents in the new development from the very beginning. A parent who is asked to observe and record exactly what happens in aspects of classroom life will surely see the real situation, will believe in the improvements, will feel part of the development and will realise what an incredibly difficult job teaching is. Possibly a parent and an older child could record the data together.

What exactly do we need to record? Overleaf are some important points:

INFANT

1 The length of time each child remains in the book corner. Do a study at intervals over three days.

2 The length of time individual children are seen to be engaged with one book in any one reading. Use 10 children as a sample.

3 The amount of reading done in different contexts by three children in a day. This is very difficult since it is hard to tell when someone is reading notices or lists. However, a simple observation of the total amount of reading will offer a comparison for the future.

4 The number of times a child asks for help from you. Take four half-day samples.

5 The length of time that children are seen reading to their peers during a morning. Take samples over a period of four mornings.

6 The number of children who choose reading when given a choice of activity. Take 10 sample visits.

7 The number of books on the floor or discarded in other inappropriate ways at any one time. Take 10 sample visits.

8 The volume of writing. Keep some samples of individual children's writing over a period of one week. Remember where you put it.

9 The number of parents choosing a book with their child. This is different from being given a book by a teacher. Take a sample over a week of morning or evenings.

10 The number of children who seem to feel that they cannot read. This is very difficult and very subjective. Occasionally, children will say that they cannot read, but even if they won't admit it, they will usually do things which indicate that they are not feeling part of the scene. They will rarely choose a book, they will avoid sharing a book with an adult, they will lose their book, they will go AWOL when it is their turn to read to the teacher, they will say they do not like books or they will forget to take their book home.

All of these observations can relate to the infant classroom and will offer information on the progress of development within the age group. There is another facet though. We need to see the long-term effects of our action upon children as they grow up into the junior stage and into adult readership. Perhaps, at this early stage we should record the same aspects of the readership of our junior children so that we can assess whether the effects of our developing approach with young readers is actually helping the children learn to read and become the type of reader we want them to be.

JUNIOR

The same 10 observations will relate to the junior age group. If you observe the situation over a three-week period now, next year and the year after with a middle or older junior group, you will gain a picture of the impact and results of your efforts.

None of these records are scientific or final pieces of evidence. What they offer is a chance to look back at progress. By repeating the process, under the same sample conditions, at set dates, the picture of development can be built up so that what is measured in terms of progress is what we actually thought was important at the beginning.

Store the information away carefully. Remember where it is stored! Enter some dates in the diary to carry out the same observations again. Set about the new developments.

Choosing books for beginner readers

This is by no means a comprehensive list—everyone has his or her own favourites.

AHLBERG, JANET AND ALLEN, *Peepo!*, Penguin 1983
  The baby's catalogue, Penguin 1984
BRIGGS, RAYMOND, *Mother Goose treasury*, Penguin 1973
BUCKNALL, CAROLINE, *One bear all alone*, Macmillan 1987.
BURNINGHAM, JOHN, *The blanket*, Jonathan Cape 1975
CAMPBELL, ROD, *Dear zoo*, Campbell Blackie 1987
  Oh dear, Blackie 1983
CARLE, ERIC, *The bad-tempered ladybird*, Penguin 1982
  The very busy spider, Hamish Hamilton 1985 (out of print)
  The very hungry caterpillar, Penguin 1974
CROWTHER, ROBERT, *The most amazing hide and seek alphabet book*, Viking Kestral 1978
GARLAND, SARAH, *Doing the washing*, Penguin 1985
  Going shopping, Penguin 1985
  Having a picnic, Penguin 1985
GINSBURG, MIRRA AND BARTON, BYRON, *Good morning Chick*, MacRae Books 1980
  AND TAFURI, NANCY, *Across the stream*, Penguin 1985
GRETZ, SUSANNA, *Teddy bears one to ten*, Collins 1973
HILL, ERIC, *Spot goes to the circus*, Heinemann 1986
  Spot's birthday party, Baker Book Services 1987
  Spot's first walk, Baker Book Services 1987
  Where's Spot?, Baker Book Services 1987
HUGHES, SHIRLEY, *Lucy and Tom's ABC*, Penguin 1986
HUTCHINS, PAT, *Goodnight, Owl*, Penguin 1975
  Rosie's walk, Bodley Head 1987
  Titch, Penguin 1974
  You'll soon grow into them, Titch, Penguin 1985
  1 Hunter, Penguin 1984
MARIS, RON, *Are you there, Bear?*, Penguin 1986
  Better move on, Frog, Armada Books 1984
  Is anyone home?, Penguin 1987
  My book, Penguin 1985
MARTIN, BILL AND CARLE, ERIC, *Brown Bear, Brown Bear. What did you see?*, Armada Books 1986

MCKEE, DAVID, *Not now, Bernard*, Ingham Yates 1987
MURPHY, JILL, *Peace at last*, Macmillan 1987
ORMEROD, JAN, *Sunshine*, Penguin 1983
    Moonlight, Kestrel Books 1982
OXENBURY, HELEN, *Nursery-story book*, Heinemann 1985
PRATER, JOHN, *On Friday something funny happened*, Penguin 1984
TAFURI, NANCY, *Have you seen my duckling?*, Penguin 1986
TOLSTOY, ALEXEI AND OXENBURY, HELEN, *The great big enormous turnip*,
    Armada Books 1988
VOAKE, CHARLOTTE, *Over the moon. A book of nursery rhymes*, Walker
    Books 1985 (out of print)
WATANABE, SHIGEO, *How do I eat it?*, Penguin 1982
    Ready, steady, go!, Bodley Head 1981
    How do I put it on?, Bodley Head 1986

There is an increasing number of big books with accompanying copies
in normal size. These are particularly suited for an adult or experienced
reader to read with a group or a class. Here are two examples of this
kind of series:
Readalong rhythms series, Mary Glasgow Publications
Giant magic bean books, Era publications (div. of RD Martin, Australia)

Reading together one to one

For teachers
BLOOM, WENDY, *Partnership with parents in reading*, Hodder & Stoughton
    1987
BRANSTON, PETER AND PROVIS, MARK, *CAPER* (Children and parents
    enjoying reading), Hodder & Stoughton 1986
GRIFFITHS AND HAMILTON, *Parent, teacher, child*, Methuen 1985
HANNON, PETER, ETC, *Involving parents in the teaching of reading*,
    University of Sheffield 1985
JACKSON, ANGELA AND HANNON, PETER, *Belfield Reading Project final
    report*, Belfield Community Council/National Children's Bureau 1987
MORGAN, ROGER, *Helping children read: the paired reading handbook*,
    Methuen 1986
PITFIELD PROJECT, *Home-school reading partnership in Hackney*, ILEA 1984
PRITCHARD, DAVID AND RENNIEL, JOHN, *Reading: involving parents*,
    Community Education Development Centre (CEDC), Coventry 1978
TOPPING, KEITH AND WOLFENDALE, S (EDS), *Parental involvement in
    children's reading*, Croom Helm 1985
WATERLAND, LIZ, *Read with me*, Thimble Press 1985
WIDLAKE, PAUL AND MCCLEOD, FLORA, *Raising standards*, CEDC,
    Coventry 1984

For parents
BUTLER, DOROTHY, *Babies need books*, Penguin 1982 (out of print)
    Five to eight, Bodley Head 1986

CENTRE FOR LANGUAGE IN PRIMARY EDUCATION (CLPE), *Read, read, read*, ILEA 1979

MEEK, MARGARET, *Learning to read*, Bodley Head 1986

TAYLOR, BING AND BRAITHWAITE, PETER, *"Good book guide" to children's books*, Penguin 1986

TRELEASE, JIM, *The read aloud handbook*, Penguin 1984 (out of print)

Video

Hertford Media (formerly Chiltern Consortium), *Partners in reading*

Coventry Community Education Project, *Home reading/learning packs*

References

1. DES Committee of Enquiry, *Bullock report: Language for Life*, HMSO 1975
2. DES, *English from 5 to 16* (2nd ed), HMSO 1986
3. Wells, Gordon, *The meaning makers*, Hodder & Stoughton 1987
4. Smith, Frank, *Reading* (2nd ed), Cambridge University Press 1986
5. Donaldson, Margaret, *Children's minds*, Fontana 1984
6. Inglis, F, *The promise of happiness*, Cambridge University Press 1982
7. Bawden, Nina, *The peppermint pig*, Chivers Press 1987
8. Pearce, Philippa, *Tom's midnight garden*, Windrush 1987
9. Peters, Margaret, 'Purposeful Writing', in Raban, Bridie (ed), *Practical ways to teach writing*, Ward Lock 1985
10. Bennett, Jill, *Learning to read with picture books*, Thimble Press 1985
11. Maris, Ron, *Better move on, Frog*, Armada Books 1984
12. Graves, Donald, *Writing: teachers and children at work*, Heinemann 1983
13. *About writing*, newsletter of the National Writing Project, School Curriculum Development Committee
14. *Language matters*, published three times a year by the Centre for Language in Primary Education (CLPE)
15. Hutchins, Pat, *Rosie's walk*, Bodley Head 1987
16. Hall, Nigel, *The emergence of literacy*, Hodder & Stoughton 1987
17. Gipps, C et al, *Testing children*, Heinemann 1983 (out of print)
18. Daniels, J C and Diack, H, 'Graded test of reading experience', *The standard reading tests*, Chatto & Windus 1958
19. Jackson, Angela and Hannon, Peter, *Belfield Reading Project final report*, Belfield Community Council/National Children's Bureau 1987
20. Waterland, Liz, *Read with me*, Thimble Press 1985
21. Hill, Eric, *Spot's first walk*, Baker Book Services 1987
22. McKee, David, *Not now, Bernard*, Ingham Yates 1987
23. Hughes, Ted, *The Iron Man*, Faber 1985
24. Nimmo, Jenny, *The snow spider*, Magnet Books 1987
25. Magorian, Michelle, *Goodnight Mr Tom*, Penguin 1983
26. Aiken, Joan, *The wolves of Willoughby Chase*, Chivers Press 1986
27. Garner, Alan, *The weirdstone of Brisingamen*, Collins 1971
28. Hutchins, Pat, *Rosie's walk*, Bodley Head 1987
29. Sendak, Maurice, *Where the wild things are*, Penguin 1970
30. Burningham, John, *Come away from the water, Shirley*, Armada Books 1983

1994

4

1997